The Government of the Tongue

SEAMUS HEANEY

The Government of the Tongue

SELECTED PROSE

1978–1987

The Noonday Press

Farrar, Straus and Giroux

New York

For Charles Monteith

Contents

Acknowledgements

The second part of this book consists of the T. S. Eliot Memorial Lectures, delivered in October 1986 at Eliot College, in the University of Kent. I am grateful to Dr Shirley Barlow, Master of Eliot College, for her hospitality to my wife and myself on that occasion, which was made memorable also by the presence in the audience of Mrs Valerie Eliot; and of many friends including, in particular, the dedicatee, Charles Monteith, erstwhile assistant to T. S. Eliot, and my first editor at Faber and Faber.

The first part is made up of pieces written for or delivered upon various occasions. The introductory essay steals from 'Place and Displacement', originally presented as the first Pete Laver Memorial Lecture at Grasmere in 1984, and from a lecture given to the Royal Dublin Society in 1986, subsequently printed in *Shenandoah* as 'The Interesting Case of Nero, Chekhov's Cognac and a Knocker'. 'The Placeless Heaven' was the opening address at Kavanagh's Yearly, at Carrickmacross in November 1985, and was afterwards printed in the *Massachusetts Review*. 'The Main of Light' appeared in *Larkin at Sixty* (Faber, 1982). 'The Murmur of Malvern' (originally entitled 'The Language of Exile'), 'The Fully Exposed Poem' and 'Atlas of Civilization' were published as review articles in *Parnassus*. 'The Poems of the Dispossessed Repossessed' appeared in the *Sunday Tribune*. 'Sounding Auden' and 'Osip and Nadezhda Mandelstam' were published in the *London Review of Books*. 'The Impact of Translation' was a contribution to the 1986 conference of the English Institute and was printed in the *Yale Review*. 'Lowell's Command' appeared in *Salmagundi*.

In the course of the first of the Eliot Memorial Lectures, I pirated a few pages from my 'Envies and Identifications: Dante and the Modern Poet' (*Irish University Review*, Spring, 1985); and in the course of the third one, I culled sentences from my contribution to the 1979 MLA symposium on 'Current Unstated Assumptions About Poetry' (*Critical Inquiry*, Summer, 1981). Every one of the pieces has undergone revisions, mostly for stylistic reasons, but sometimes in order to shed material more appropriate to the original occasion than to the context of this book.

I am indebted as ever to friends and colleagues: Helen Vendler, Frank Bidart and Bernard McCabe read several parts of the manuscript and helped me to get some things into more exact language. To Nancy Williston, who performed the feat of transmitting the contents of innumerable rewritten, handwritten pages into the serviceable memory of a word-processor, I am grateful for unfailing good humour and valiant persistence at the keyboard.

The Interesting Case of Nero, Chekhov's Cognac and a Knocker

In 1972, in Belfast, I had an arrangement one evening to meet my friend, the singer David Hammond. We were to assemble in a recording studio in order to put together a tape of songs and poems for a mutual friend in Michigan. The tape was to be sent in memory of a party which the man from Michigan had attended some months beforehand, when tunes and staves had been uttered with great conviction. The occasion had been immensely enjoyable and the whole point of the tape was to promote that happiness and expansiveness which song, meaning both poetry and music, exists to promote in the first place.

In the event, we did not actually make the tape. On our way to the studio, a number of explosions occurred in the city and the air was full of the sirens of ambulances and fire engines. There was news of casualties. A certain half-directed fury was evident behind the ministrations of the loyalist BBC security men who checked us in. There was no sense of what to anticipate. And still that implacable disconsolate wailing of the ambulances continued.

It was music against which the music of the guitar that David unpacked made little impression. So little, indeed, that the very notion of beginning to sing at that moment when others were beginning to suffer seemed like an offence against their suffering. He could not raise his voice at that cast-down moment. He packed the guitar again and we both drove off into the destroyed evening.

I begin with this story because it dramatizes a tension which is the underlying subject of many of the pieces in this book. It is a tension to which all artists are susceptible, just as the children of temperamentally opposed parents are susceptible. The child in this case is the poet, and the parents are called Art and Life. Both Art and Life have had a hand in the formation of any poet, and both are to be loved, honoured and obeyed. Yet both are often perceived to be in conflict and that conflict is constantly and sympathetically suffered by the poet. He or she begins to feel that a choice between the two, a once-and-for-all option, would simplify things. Deep down, of course, there is the sure awareness that no such simple solution or dissolution is possible, but the waking mind desires constantly some clarified allegiance, without complication or ambivalence.

Perhaps Art and Life sound a little distant, so let us put it more melodramatically and call them Song and Suffering. What David Hammond and I were experiencing, at a most immediate and obvious level, was a feeling that song constituted a betrayal of suffering. To go back even further to an archetypal if cartoonish version of the same situation: if we had played and sung and said poems, we would have been following the example of the singer and player Nero, who notoriously fiddled while Rome burned. Nero's action has ever since been held up as an example of human irresponsibility, if not callousness; conventionally, it represents an abdication from the usual instinctive need which a human being feels in such situations to lament, if not to try to prevent, the fate of the stricken; proverbially, it has come to stand for actions which are frivolous to the point of effrontery, and useless to the point of insolence. Nobody has a good word to say for Nero, it would seem. And nobody, it would seem, could blame Hammond and myself for clamming up in earshot of the sirens: to have sung and said the poems in those conditions would have been a culpable indulgence.

Or would it? Why should the joyful affirmation of music and poetry ever constitute an affront to life? One answer is, of course, that there can be a complacency and an insulation from reality in some song and some art, which in itself constitutes the affront. This perception – of the mystification which Art can involve – was notoriously enforced upon those poets who experienced the gap between reality and rhetoric in the trenches of Flanders during the First World War, and it is from this moment in our century that radiant and unperturbed certitudes about the consonance between the true and the beautiful become suspect. The *locus classicus* for all this is in the life and poetry of Wilfred Owen, the young English poet who died at the front in 1918. Ever since Edmund Blunden published his edition of the poems and his memoir of Owen in 1931, this brave and tender poet has haunted the back of the literary mind as a kind of challenge. The challenge is voiced simply by Geoffrey Hill in these lines:

> Must men stand by what they write
> as by their camp beds or their weaponry
> or shell-shocked comrades while they sag and cry?

The fact that Hill's question is couched in terms of a First World War vocabulary makes it all the more apposite. Should you write something you are not prepared to live or, *in extremis*, die for? What did Horace mean when he wrote the lines *dulce et decorum est pro patria mori*? It is sweet and right to die for your fatherland? What, Owen asks even more savagely, does the twentieth-century poet mean who repeats this kind of consoling and mystifying rhetoric at a safe distance from the front where the actual dying takes place? His poems were meant to outrage rather than console. They were written out of the shock of the deception incurred by conventional artistic expression – in particular, the expression of the notion that dying for your country is beautiful. In a preface which would not see the light until after his own death a week before armistice in 1918, Owen affirmed that his poems would have nothing to do with this complacent, acceptable version of the beautiful which he contemptuously calls 'Poetry'. The whole thing is passionately anti-heroic:

> This book is not about heroes. English poetry is not yet fit to speak of them.
> Nor is it about deeds, or lands, nor anything about glory, honour, might, majesty, dominion, or power, except War.
> Above all I am not concerned with Poetry.
> My subject is War, and the pity of War.

The Poetry is in the pity.
Yet these elegies are to this generation in no sense
consolatory. They may be to the next. All a poet can do
today is warn. That is why the true Poets must be
truthful . . .

And what exactly this truthfulness demands can be seen in
the violent assault he makes upon the genteel citadel of English
pastoral verse in lines like these:

> If in some smothering dreams you too could pace
> Behind the wagon that we flung him in,
> And watch the white eyes writhing in his face,
> His hanging face, like a devil's sick of sin;
> If you could hear, at every jolt, the blood
> Come gargling from the froth-corrupted lungs,
> Obscene as cancer, bitter as the cud
> Of vile, incurable sores on innocent tongues, –
> My friend, you would not tell with such high zest
> To children ardent for some desperate glory,
> The old Lie: Dulce et decorum est
> Pro patria mori.

Owen so stood by what he wrote that he seemed almost to
obliterate the line between art and life: what we might call his
sanctity is a field of force which deflects anything as privileged
as literary criticism. His poems have the potency of human
testimony, of martyr's relics, so that any intrusion of the
aesthetic can feel like impropriety. They so opt for truth that the
beauty consideration is made to seem irrelevant. I remember
feeling this very acutely when I was lecturing on the poems in
Queen's University, twenty years ago. Part of my function
there was to convince students of the power and reality of
poetry, and obviously the First World War was a wonderful
example of a moment when poets functioned as effective and
heroic figures in the life of their times. Owen was against the
violence of war, against the massive sacrilegious waste of lives
which it involved; he was a natural conscientious objector. And
yet, when he actually drilled and led men to death, he was
behaving in a way that contravened his personal conscience in

order to achieve what he saw as a greater goal, namely the awakening of a general conscience. 'True poets must be truthful.' 'All a poet can do today is warn.' These imperatives could be effectively fulfilled only if the poet who was warning or telling his truth was doing so with the authority of experience, with the justification of soldiering behind him. Owen therefore suffered the strain of performing what most people perceived to be their unquestionable patriotic duty in order to gain the right to question whether it was duty at all. He connived in what he deplored so that he could deplore what he connived in: he earned the right to his lines by going up the line, and nobody who has read Owen's poems and letters can underestimate their cost in terms of trauma and courage and heartbreak.

So it is easy to revere this poet as a kind of saintly figure, the victim, the scapegoat, the paradoxically gentle man of violence, with a machine-gun in one hand and a *mea culpa* in the other. And revering him so, as a figure of courage, somebody whose moral substance makes the rest of us feel like moral shadows, it seems like an impertinence when we begin to do what I occasionally did in those lectures twenty years ago – to make pejorative critical remarks about the excessively vehement adjectives and nouns in the lines of Owen's which I have quoted. Here, again, was that moment of crucial encounter between art and life. And here, again, the artistic consideration, the need to call for verbal restraint, felt prissy and trivial when you considered what lay behind the words. Nevertheless, I was not only concerned that the socio-political testimony of poets be apprehended by the students; I was also concerned with what was artistically good as well as what was generally true. And it seemed to me that *Dulce Et Decorum Est*, a poem which it was easy for them to like, was the poem where I could engage them with the question of over-writing. 'Is Owen overdoing it here?' I would ask. 'Inside five lines we have "devil's sick of sin", "gargling", "froth-corrupted", "bitter as the cud", "vile, incurable sores". Is he not being a bit over-insistent? A bit explicit?' However hangdog I might feel about such intrusions, I also felt that it was right to raise questions. Yet there was obviously an immense disparity between the nit-picking criticism I was conducting on the poem and the heavy price, in terms of emotional and physical suffering, the poet paid in order to bring it into being.

Wilfred Owen, and others like him in the trenches of Flanders, are among the first of a type of poet who increasingly appears in the annals of twentieth-century literature, and who looms as a kind of shadowy judging figure above every poet who has written subsequently. The shorthand name we have evolved for this figure is the 'poet as witness', and he represents poetry's solidarity with the doomed, the deprived, the victimized, the under-privileged. The witness is any figure in whom the truth-telling urge and the compulsion to identify with the oppressed becomes necessarily integral with the act of writing itself.

It has, of course, been the tragic destiny of several writers in the Soviet Union and the Eastern bloc countries to feel this 'call to witness' more extremely than most others. Yet one has only to think of the Scottish Gaelic poet, Sorley MacLean, in the 1930s, enduring agonies of conscience about whether or not he, as socialist and poet, should be in Spain fighting with the international brigades in the Civil War, to realize that no poet is spared the consciousness of these great exemplary lives. Not even the shelter of a marginal homeland in the Hebrides or a minority language could keep out the demands of the age. MacLean felt that his rights to exercise his lyric gift and his duty to the wretched of the earth at that critical Spanish moment were somehow related. The line between song and suffering could be obliterated by the poet's expiatory, committed action.

The psychology of this is completely understandable, and it was at work also in the case of Chekhov when he visited a penal colony in the 1890s, to record the conditions under which the prisoners lived, to live with them, interview them and subsequently publish a book about his experiences. Here Chekhov was, as it were, establishing his rights to write imaginatively, earning the free joy of his fiction by the hard facts of his sociological report. Significantly, he called his trip to the penal colony his 'debt to medicine', betraying thereby a characteristic modesty and prophetically modern guilt about the act of creative writing itself. The medical man in him was obviously the one whom he somehow regarded as possessing rights to a space in the world, while the writer had to earn that space, had to earn the right to the luxury of practising his art. It is all beautifully summed up in the spectacle of Chekhov, on his first night on that prison island of Sakhalin, getting drunk on a bottle of cognac.

Months earlier, in Moscow, his friends had been astonished at his determination to make the awful journey in the first place; Sakhalin was then a kind of Devil's Island where the sweepings of Russian society, criminals and decadents of all sorts, were banished along with others whom society did not want to be bothered with, political prisoners and agitators. Chekhov, despite his newly found position in the world as an artistic and social success, was determined – oddly determined, as far as the Moscow *literati* were concerned – to go through with the expedition. This was partly because of his consciously adhered-to beliefs about the necessity to work for a good and just future and partly, no doubt, because of his unconscious identification of something in himself with his serf grandfather. It was this oppressed shadow-self, with whom he was compelled to struggle, that he hoped to lay to rest on the island of Sakhalin. Once, he had declared that he had squeezed the final drop of slave's blood out of himself and wakened up at last a free man. That, if you like, was a conscious declaration of intent. The Sakhalin journey would be a half-conscious ritual of exorcism of the slave's blood in him and an actual encompassing of psychic and artistic freedom; it would be a bid for 'inner freedom', 'the feeling of being right', as his countryman, Osip Mandelstam, would call it forty years later.

At any rate, to the bewilderment of his friends in the salons of the capital, Anton Chekhov set out upon his long journey to the prisons of Sakhalin in the summer of 1890 and, as a parting gift, those friends presented him with a bottle of cognac. This he preserved during his long and difficult six weeks' journey by coach and boat, until he broached and drank it on his first night on the island. I have often thought of that as an emblematic moment: the writer taking his pleasure in the amber cognac, savouring a fume of intoxication and a waft of luxury in the stink of oppression and the music of cruelty – on Sakhalin he could literally hear the chink of convicts' chains. Let the cognac represent not just the gift of his friends but the gift of his art, and here we have an image of the poet appeased; justified and unabashed by the suffering which surrounds him because unflinchingly responsible to it.

In Chekhov, in Owen, in Sorley MacLean, we find the impulse to elevate truth above beauty, to rebuke the sovereign claims which art would make for itself, caricatured in the figure of Nero, the singer and player culpably absorbed in his melodies while his city burns around him. In them, we find examples of that embarrassment, symbolized by David Hammond's refusal to sing, which the poet may find as he exercises his free gift in the presence of the unfree and the hurt. When I say free gift, I mean that lyric poetry, however responsible, always has an element of the untrammelled about it. There is a certain jubilation and truancy at the heart of an inspiration. There is a sensation of liberation and abundance which is the antithesis of every hampered and deprived condition. And it is for this reason that, psychologically, the lyric poet feels the need for justification in a world that is notably hampered and deprived.

This embarrassment of the poet because of the artfulness of his art is nowhere more apparent than in the post-war poetry of Eastern Europe, in particular the poetry of Poland. If Wilfred Owen, in the relatively innocent hand-to-hand conditions of the trenches, could feel that poetry was an offence – 'above all I am not concerned with Poetry' – how much more offensive it was bound to seem to those Polish survivors of Nazi horror and Holocaust, and Soviet cynicism. Anti-poetry was all they were prepared to deal with. In the words of Zbigniew Herbert, the task of the poet now was 'to salvage out of the catastrophe of history at least two words, without which all poetry is an empty play of meanings and appearances, namely: justice and truth'. It is no wonder then to find Zbigniew Herbert writing a lyric whose ostensible function is to abjure the quality of lyricism altogether. The poem (which I discuss on pages 99–100) is called, simply, 'A Knocker', and would appear to be standing up for the down-to-earthness of life against the flighty, carried-away fantasies of art. And yet Herbert is content enough to allow art its rights provided it knows its limitations. 'Go in peace,' his poem says. 'Enjoy poetry as long as you don't use it to escape reality.' It gives absolution to poet and audience alike, provided that true penitence, namely an abjuration of poetry as self-indulgent ornament, has occurred. In other words, I am inclined to think that if Herbert had been in the studio with us in 1972, he would have encouraged us to stay and make the tape.

Did we not see that song and poetry added to the volume of good in the world? he might have asked. Could we not remember the example of Mandelstam, singing in the Stalinist night, affirming the essential humanism of the act of poetry itself against the inhuman tyranny which would have had him write odes not just to Stalin but to hydro-electric dams? As opposed to these prescribed and propagandist themes, the essential thing about lyric poetry, Mandelstam maintained, was its unlooked-for joy in being itself, and the essential thing for the lyric poet was therefore a condition in which he was in thrall to no party or programme, but truly and freely and utterly himself. Unlike Chekhov, who wrote on behalf of the prisoners explicitly, and unlike Owen, who had a messianic and socially redemptive message to impart, Mandelstam had no immediate social aim. Utterance itself was self-justifying and creative, like nature.

Mandelstam implied that it was the poet's responsibility to allow poems to form in language inside him, the way crystals formed in a chemical solution. He was the vessel of language. His responsibility was to sound rather than to the state, to phonetics rather than to five-year plans, to etymology rather than to economics. Mandelstam wanted to give himself over to his creative processes without the interference of his own self-censorship or the imposition of Soviet orthodoxy. For him, obedience to poetic impulse was obedience to conscience; lyric action constituted radical witness. Even though in the meantime we have become highly conscious of the conditioning nature of language itself, the way it speaks us as much as we speak it, the essential point remains: Mandelstam's witness to the necessity of what he called 'breathing freely', even at the price of his death; to the art of poetry as an unharnessed, non-didactic, non-party-dictated, inspired act.

So if Owen sponsors an art which seems to rebuke beauty in

favour of truth, Mandelstam, at an equally high price, sponsors all over again the Keatsian proposition that beauty *is* truth, truth beauty. He is a burning reminder of the way in which not only the words 'truth' and 'justice' may be salvaged from the catastrophe of history, but the word 'beauty' also: a reminder that humanity is served by the purely poetic fidelity of the poet to all words in their pristine being, in 'the steadfastness of their speech articulation'. Mandelstam died because he could not suppress his urge to sing in his own way. It so happened that he had no anti-Communist sentiments to voice, but nevertheless, because he would not change his tune as the Kremlin required, he represented a threat to the power of the tyrant and had to go. He therefore stands for the efficacy of song itself, an emblem of the poet as potent sound-wave; and when one thinks of the note of the soprano which cracks glass, one has yet another image of the way purely artistic utterance can put a crack into the officially moulded shape of truth in a totalitarian society.

In the course of this book, Mandelstam and other poets from Eastern bloc countries are often invoked. I keep returning to them because there is something in their situation that makes them attractive to a reader whose formative experience has been largely Irish. There is an unsettled aspect to the different worlds they inhabit, and one of the challenges they face is to survive amphibiously, in the realm of 'the times' and the realm of their moral and artistic self-respect, a challenge immediately recognizable to anyone who has lived with the awful and demeaning facts of Northern Ireland's history over the last couple of decades.

The relative absence of Irish subjects from this selection does not therefore mean lack of interest in what is happening in poetry on the home front or in what is being made of it. A literary and political discourse has been generated, a cultural debate is proceeding, yet much of it is drawn upon the work of poets, playwrights and novelists who have been one's companions and respected seniors for over a quarter of a century. As a consequence, the debate toils through much that was already, in the beginning, *déjà entendu*. When John Hewitt and John Montague, for example, toured Northern Ireland in 1970 with a programme of readings from their poems called *The Planter and the Gael*, the fact that it was an Arts Council tour and yet bore that particular title did represent a certain amelioration of local conditions. The monosyllable, Gael, was an admission in the official language of Unionist Ulster that there was a Gaelic dimension to Ulsterness – something that would have been taboo in the six counties of Lord Brookborough where I grew up in the 1940s and 1950s. Indeed, that programme was itself symptomatic of a general attempt being made at the time to bring the solvent of concepts like 'heritage', 'traditions' and 'history' into play in the foreclosed arenas of culture and politics. It was a palliative, true in its way, but as everybody including the poets knew, it was not the whole truth.

Like other members of the population, young and old, the poets knew the score. Sectarian prejudice, discrimination in jobs and housing, gerrymandering by the majority, a shared understanding that the police were a paramilitary force – all this was recognized as deplorable, and yet it would be fair to say that by the mid-1960s there was a nascent expectation of better things, on both sides. Obviously the old guard would not easily or willingly have yielded advantage or changed its ways, but with a more active and vocal Civil Rights movement at work, and a less blatantly triumphalist generation of Unionist politicians emerging, an evolution towards a better, juster internal balance might have been half trusted to begin.

I think the writers of my generation saw themselves as part of the leaven. The fact that a literary action was afoot was itself a new political condition, and the poets did not feel the need to address themselves to the specifics of politics because they assumed that the tolerances and subtleties of their art were precisely what they had to set against the repetitive intolerance of public life. When Derek Mahon, Michael Longley, James Simmons and myself were having our first book published, Paisley was already in full sectarian cry and Northern Ireland's cabinet ministers regularly massaged the atavisms of Orangemen on the Twelfth of July. Hair-raising bigotries were propounded and reported in the press as a matter of course and not a matter for comment. Nothing in the situation needed to be exposed since it was all entirely barefaced. It seemed, rather, that conditions had to be outstripped and it is tempting to view the whole syndrome in the light of Jung's thesis that an insoluble conflict is overcome by outgrowing it, developing in the process a 'new level of consciousness'. This development involves detachment from one's emotions:

> One certainly does feel the affect and is tormented by it, yet at the same time one is aware of a higher consciousness looking on which prevents one from becoming identified with the affect, a consciousness which regards the affect as an object, and can say 'I know that I suffer'.

'The affect' means a disturbance, a warp in the emotional glass which is in danger of narrowing the mind's range of response to the terms of the disturbance itself. In our case, this affect rose from the particular exacerbations attendant on being natives and residents of Northern Ireland at that time. By the 1960s, in Jung's scenario, 'a higher consciousness' was manifesting itself in the form of poetry itself, an ideal towards which the poets turned in order to survive the stunting conditions.

The achievement of a poem, after all, is an experience of release. In that liberated moment, when the lyric discovers its buoyant completion and the timeless formal pleasure comes to fullness and exhaustion, something occurs which is equidistant from self-justification and self-obliteration. A plane is – fleetingly – established where the poet is intensified in his being and freed from his predicaments. The tongue, governed for so long in the social sphere by considerations of tact and fidelity, by nice obeisances to one's origin within the minority or the majority, this tongue is suddenly ungoverned. It gains access to a condition that is unconstrained and, while not being practically effective, is not necessarily inefficacious.

The following pages rehearse again the truth of these propositions about poetry. Yet they are also symptomatic of an anxiety that in arrogating to oneself the right to take refuge in form, one is somehow denying the claims of the beggar at the gate. Writing these essays helped to allay this worry and to verify what I believe anyhow: that poetry can be as potentially redemptive and possibly as illusory as love. They encompass in prose a conviction which got expressed a decade ago in a poem called 'The Singer's House'. I wrote it for David Hammond after the event described at the beginning of this introduction and I would once again cite its concluding stanzas as a point of repose and as a point of departure:

> People here used to believe
> that drowned souls lived in seals.
> At spring tides they might change shape.
> They loved music and swam in for a singer
>
> who might stand at the end of summer
> in the mouth of a whitewashed turf-shed,
> his shoulder to the jamb, his song
> a rowboat far out in evening.
>
> When I came here first you were always singing,
> a hint of the clip of the pick
> in your winnowing climb and attack.
> Raise it again, man. We still believe what we hear.

[*I*]

The Placeless Heaven:
Another Look at Kavanagh

In 1939, the year that Patrick Kavanagh arrived in Dublin, an aunt of mine planted a chestnut in a jam jar. When it began to sprout she broke the jar, made a hole and transplanted the thing under a hedge in front of the house. Over the years, the seedling shot up into a young tree that rose taller and taller above the boxwood hedge. And over the years I came to identify my own life with the life of the chestnut tree.

This was because everybody remembered and constantly repeated the fact that it had been planted the year I was born; also because I was something of a favourite with that particular aunt, so her affection came to be symbolized in the tree; and also perhaps because the chestnut was the one significant thing that grew as I grew. The rest of the trees and hedges round the house were all mature and appeared therefore like given features of the world: the chestnut tree, on the other hand, was young and was watched in much the same way as the other children and myself were watched and commented upon, fondly, frankly and unrelentingly.

When I was in my early teens, the family moved away from that house and the new owners of the place eventually cut down every tree around the yard and the lane and the garden, including the chestnut tree. We deplored all that, of course, but life went on satisfactorily enough where we resettled, and for years I gave no particular thought to the place we had left or to my tree which had been felled. Then, all of a sudden, a couple of years ago, I began to think of the space where the tree had been or would have been. In my mind's eye I saw it as a kind of luminous emptiness, a warp and waver of light, and once again, in a way that I find hard to define, I began to identify

[3]

with that space just as years before I had identified with the young tree.

Except that this time it was not so much a matter of attaching oneself to a living symbol of being rooted in the native ground; it was more a matter of preparing to be unrooted, to be spirited away into some transparent, yet indigenous afterlife. The new place was all idea, if you like; it was generated out of my experience of the old place but it was not a topographical location. It was and remains an imagined realm, even if it can be located at an earthly spot, a placeless heaven rather than a heavenly place.

In this lecture, I am going to suggest an analogy between the first tree and the last tree as I have just described them, and the early and late poetry of Patrick Kavanagh. I also want to talk about that poetry in terms of my earliest and latest responses to it. And I hope that what emerges will be not just a personal record but some kind of generally true account of the nature of Patrick Kavanagh's essential poems.

Briefly, then, I would suggest that the early Kavanagh poem starts up like my childhood tree in its home ground; it is supplied with a strong physical presence and is full of the recognitions which existed between the poet and his place; it is symbolic of affections rooted in a community life and has behind it an imagination which is not yet weaned from its origin, an attached rather than a detached faculty, one which lives, to use Kavanagh's own metaphor, in a fog. Many of those early poems do indeed celebrate the place as heavenly, many more are disappointed that it is not as heavenly as it could or should be, but all of the early Monaghan poetry gives the place credit for existing, assists at its real topographical presence, dwells upon it and accepts it as the definitive locus of the given world.

The horizons of the little fields and hills, whether they are gloomy and constricting or radiant and enhancing, are sensed as the horizons of consciousness. Within those horizons, however, the poet who utters the poems is alive and well as a sharp critical intelligence. He knows that the Monaghan world is not the whole world, yet it is the only one for him, the one which he embosses solidly and intimately into the words of poems. We might say that Kavanagh is pervious to this world's spirit more than it is pervious to his spirit. When the Big Forth of Rocksavage is mentioned, or Cassidy's Hanging Hill, the reader senses immediately that these are places in the actual countryside which are pressing constantly into memory. In this early period, the experienced physical reality of Monaghan life imposes itself upon the poet's consciousness so that he necessarily composes himself, his poetic identity and his poems in relation to that encircling horizon of given experience.

In the poetry of Kavanagh's later period, embodied first in 'Epic' and then, in the late 1950s, in the Canal Bank Sonnets, a definite change is perceptible. We might say that now the world is more pervious to his vision than he is pervious to the world. When he writes about places now, they are luminous spaces within his mind. They have been evacuated of their status as background, as documentary geography, and exist instead as transfigured images, sites where the mind projects its own force. In this later poetry, place is included within the horizon of Kavanagh's mind rather than the other way around. The country he visits is inside himself:

> I do not know what age I am,
> I am no mortal age;
> I know nothing of women,
> Nothing of cities,
> I cannot die
> Unless I walk outside these whitethorn hedges.
>
> ('Innocence')

At the edge of consciousness in a late poem such as that, we encounter the white light of meditation; at the edge of consciousness in the early poems, the familiar world stretches reliably away. At the conclusion of poems like 'Spraying the Potatoes' and 'A Christmas Childhood', self is absorbed by scene:

> And poet lost to potato-fields,
> Remembering the lime and copper smell

> Of the spraying barrels he is not lost
> Or till blossomed stalks cannot weave a spell.

An opposite process, however, is at work at the conclusion of 'Canal Bank Walk'. Here the speaker's presence does not disperse itself in a dying fall, nor does the circumference of circumstances crowd out the perceiving centre. Even though the voice is asking to be 'enraptured', there is no hint of passivity. The rhythm heaves up strongly, bespeaking the mind's adequacy to the task of making this place – or any place – into an 'important place'. Pretending to be the world's servant, Kavanagh is actually engaged in the process of world mastery:

> O unworn world enrapture me, encapture me in a web
> Of fabulous grass and eternal voices by a beech,
> Feed the gaping need to my sense, give me ad lib
> To pray unselfconsciously with overflowing speech
> For this soul needs to be honoured with a new dress woven
> From green and blue things and arguments that cannot be
>   proven.

Similarly, in the pivotal sonnet, 'Epic', even though the poem gives the stage over to two Monaghan farmers and successfully sets Ballyrush and Gortin in balance against Munich, it is not saying that the farmers and the Monaghan region are important in themselves. They are made important only by the light of the mind which is now playing upon them. It is a poem more in praise of Kavanagh's idea of Homer than in praise of Kavanagh's home.

'Epic' appeared in the volume called *Come Dance with Kitty Stobbling*, published in 1960 and reprinted three times within the next year. My own copy is one of the fourth impression, and I have dated it 3 July 1963. I did not have many copies of books by living poets at that time and it is hard now to retrieve the sense of being on the outside of things, of being far away from 'the City of Kings/Where art music, letters are the real thing'. Belfast at that time had no literary publishers, no poetry readings, no sense of a literary identity. In 1962, while a student at St Joseph's College of Education, I had done an extended

[6]

essay on the history of literary magazines in Ulster, as though I were already seeking a basis for faith in the possibility of our cultural existence as northern, Irish and essentially ourselves. It comes as something of a shock nowadays to remember that during four years as an undergraduate in the Queen's University English Department I had not ever been taught by an Irish or an Ulster voice. I had, however, heard Louis MacNeice read his poems there and in 1963 had also listened to Thomas Kinsella read from his second volume, *Downstream*, and from earlier work. Eventually, I got my hands on Robin Skelton's anthology, *Six Irish Poets*; on the first edition of John Montague's *Poisoned Lands*, with its irrigating and confirming poem, 'The Water Carrier'; on Alvarez's anthology, *The New Poetry*, where I encountered the work of Ted Hughes and R. S. Thomas. All of these things were animating, as were occasional trips to Dublin where I managed to pick up that emblem of Ireland's quickening poetic life, *The Dolmen Miscellany of Irish Writing*, and to read in it the strong lines of Richard Murphy's 'The Cleggan Disaster'. Meanwhile, my headmaster Michael McLaverty, himself a Monaghan man by birth but with a far gentler sensibility than Kavanagh's, lent me his copy of *A Soul for Sale* and so introduced me, at the age of twenty-three, to *The Great Hunger*.

Everything, at that time, was needy and hopeful and inchoate. I had had four poems accepted for publication, two by the *Belfast Telegraph*, one by the *Irish Times* and one by *The Kilkenny Magazine*, but still, like Keats in Yeats's image, I was like a child with his nose pressed to a sweetshop window, gazing from behind a barrier at the tempting mysteries beyond. And then came this revelation and confirmation of reading Kavanagh. When I found 'Spraying the Potatoes' in the old *Oxford Book of Irish Verse*, I was excited to find details of a life which I knew intimately – but which I had always considered to be below or beyond books – being presented in a book. The barrels of blue potato spray which had stood in my own childhood like holidays of pure colour in an otherwise grey field-life – there they were, standing their ground in print. And there too was the word 'headland', which I guessed was to Kavanagh as local a word as was 'headrig' to me. Here too was the strange stillness and heat and solitude of the sunlit fields, the inexplicable melancholy of distant work-sounds, all caught in a language that was both familiar and odd:

> The axle-roll of a rut-locked cart
> Broke the burnt stick of noon in two.

And it was the same with 'A Christmas Childhood'. Once again, in the other life of print, I came upon the unregarded data of the usual life. Potato-pits with rime on them, guttery gaps, iced-over puddles being crunched, cows being milked, a child nicking the doorpost with a pen-knife, and so on. What was being experienced was not some hygienic and self-aware pleasure of the text but a primitive delight in finding world become word.

I had been hungry for this kind of thing without knowing what it was I was hungering after. For example, when I graduated in 1961, I had bought Louis MacNeice's *Collected Poems*. I did take pleasure in that work, especially in the hard-faced tenderness of something like 'Postscript from Iceland'; I recognized his warm and clinkered spirit yet I still remained at a reader's distance. MacNeice did not throw the switch that sends writing energy sizzling into a hitherto unwriting system. When I opened his book, I still came up against the window-pane of literature. His poems arose from a mind-stuff and existed in a cultural setting which were at one remove from me and what I came from. I envied them, of course, their security in the big world of history and poetry which happened out there, far beyond the world of state scholarships, the Gaelic Athletic Association, October devotions, the Clancy brothers, buckets and egg-boxes where I had had my being. I envied them but I was not taken over by them the way I was taken over by Kavanagh.

At this point, it is necessary to make one thing clear. I am not affirming here the superiority of the rural over the urban/suburban as a subject for poetry, nor am I out to sponsor deprivation at the expense of cultivation. I am not insinuating that one domain of experience is more intrinsically poetical or more ethnically desirable than another. I am trying to record exactly the sensations of one reader, from a comparatively bookless background, who came into contact with some of the established poetic voices in Ireland in the early 1960s. Needless to say, I am aware of a certain partisan strain in the criticism of Irish poetry, deriving from remarks by Samuel Beckett in the 1930s and developed most notably by Anthony Cronin. This criticism regards the vogue for poetry based on images from a country background as a derogation of literary responsibility and some sort of negative Irish feedback. It is also deliberately polemical and might be worth taking up in another context; for the moment, however, I want to keep the focus personal and look at what Kavanagh has meant to one reader, over a period of a couple of decades.

Kavanagh's genius had achieved singlehanded what I and my grammar-schooled, arts-degreed generation were badly in need of – a poetry which linked the small farm life which produced us with the slim-volume world we were now supposed to be fit for. He brought us back to what we came from. So it was natural that, to begin with, we overvalued the subject matter of the poetry at the expense of its salutary creative spirit. In the 1960s I was still more susceptible to the pathos and familiarity of the matter of Kavanagh's poetry than I was alert to the liberation and subversiveness of its manner. Instead of divesting me of my first life, it confirmed that life by giving it an image. I do not mean by that that when I read *The Great Hunger* I felt proud to have known people similar to Patrick Maguire or felt that their ethos had been vindicated. It is more that one felt less alone and marginal as a product of that world now that it had found its expression in a work which was regarded not just as part of a national culture but as a contribution to the world's store of true poems.

Kavanagh gave you permission to dwell without cultural anxiety among the usual landmarks of your life. Over the border, into a Northern Ireland dominated by the noticeably English accents of the local BBC, he broadcast a voice that would not be cowed into accents other than its own. Without being in the slightest way political in its intentions, Kavanagh's poetry did have political effect. Whether he wanted it or not, his achievement was inevitably co-opted, north and south, into the general current of feeling which flowed from and sustained ideas of national identity, cultural otherness from Britain and the dream of a literature with a manner and a matter resistant to the central Englishness of the dominant tradition. No admirer of the Irish Literary Revival, Kavanagh was read initially and almost entirely in light of the Revival writers' ambitions for a native literature.

So there I was, in 1963, with my new copy of *Come Dance with Kitty Stobbling*, in the grip of those cultural and political pieties which Kavanagh, all unknown to me, had spent the last fifteen years or so repudiating. I could feel completely at home with a poem like 'Shancoduff' – which dated from the 1930s anyhow, as did 'To the Man after the Harrow' – and with 'Kerr's Ass' and 'Ante-Natal Dream'; their imagery, after all, was continuous with the lyric poetry of the 1940s, those Monaghan rhapsodies I had known from the *Oxford Book of Irish Verse*. This was the country poet at home with his country subjects and we were all ready for that. At the time, I responded to the direct force of these later works but did not immediately recognize their visionary intent, their full spiritual daring.

To go back to our original parable, I still assumed Kavanagh to be writing about the tree which was actually in the ground when he had in fact passed on to write about the tree which he held in mind. Even a deceptively direct poem like 'In Memory of My Mother' reveals the change; this does indeed contain a catalogue of actual memories of the woman as she was and is bound to a true-life Monaghan by its images of cattle and fairdays, yet all these solidly based phenomena are transformed by a shimmer of inner reality. The poem says two things at once: mother is historically gone, mother is a visionary presence forever:

> I do not think of you lying in the wet clay
> Of a Monaghan graveyard; I see
> You walking down a lane among the poplars
> On your way to the station, or happily

> Going to second Mass on a summer Sunday –
> You meet me and you say:

'Don't forget to see about the cattle – '
Among your earthiest words the angels stray.

Though this is a relatively simple – and sentimentally threatened – manifestation of the change of focus from outer to inner reality, it does have something of that 'weightlessness' which Kavanagh came to seek as an alternative to the weightiness of the poetic substance in, say, *The Great Hunger*. It is silkier and more sinuous than the gravid powerful rough-cast of lines like:

Clay is the word and clay is the flesh
Where potato gatherers like mechanized scarecrows move
Along the sidefall of a hill, Maguire and his men.

And yet, because of its rural content, 'In Memory of My Mother' can almost pass itself off as a poem in the earlier mode. Which could not be said of lines like these, the final stanza of 'Auditors In':

From the sour soil of a town where all roots canker
I turn away to where the Self reposes
The placeless Heaven that's under all our noses
Where we're shut off from all the barren anger
No time for self-pitying melodrama
A million Instincts know no other uses
Than all day long to feed and charm the Muses
Till they become pure positive. O hunger
Where all have mouths of desire and none
Is willing to be eaten; I am so glad
To come accidentally upon
My self at the end of a tortuous road
And have learned with surprise that God
Unworshipped withers to the Futile One.

The Self, mentioned twice in those fourteen lines, is being declared the poetic arena and the poetic subject. What is important now is not so much that the world is there to be celebrated, more that the poet is at hand to proceed with the celebration. And this 'celebration' is not just a limp abstraction, a matter of religiose uplift and fine feelings. It is an altogether non-literary act, connected with what the poet began to think of as his 'comic' point of view, an abandonment of a life in order to find more abundant life.

We might say that lyric celebration was to Kavanagh what witty expression was to Oscar Wilde – in the beginning, a matter of temperament, a habit of style, a disposition of the artist's fundamental nature, but, in the end, a matter of redemptive force, a resource that maintained the artist's inner freedom in the face of worldly disappointments, an infrangible dignity. While both of them had an admitted appetite for success, neither could bear the warm breath of success once it offered itself; in order to find their lives again after what they instinctively sensed as a dangerous brush with spiritual enslavement to the group, they had to break with the terms of the group's values; they had to lose themselves. Wilde joking about wallpaper in his Paris hotel and Kavanagh walking the fields of Inniskeen, after his lung cancer operation and his traumatic libel action, are like men in a wise and unassertive afterlife.

There is enormous vigour in the new-found 'comic' conviction of the poet that he must divest himself of convictions, come to experience with the pure readiness which an angel brings to the activity of witnessing reality:

> Away, away away on wings like Joyce's
> Mother Earth is putting my brand new clothes in order
> Praying, she says, that I no more ignore her
> Yellow buttons she found in fields at bargain prices.
> Kelly's Big Bush for a button-hole. Surprises
> In every pocket – the stress at Connolly's corner
> Myself at Annavackey on Armagh border
> Or calm and collected in a calving crisis.
> Not sad at all as I float away away
> With Mother keeping me to the vernacular.
> I have a home to return to now. O blessing
> For the Return in Departure. Somewhere to stay
> Doesn't matter. What is distressing
> Is walking eagerly to go nowhere in particular.

'Walking eagerly' belonged to the old world of ego; now he is in the new world where, like the lilies of the field, he considers not his raiment nor what he will put on – Mother Earth, after all, is putting his brand new clothes in order. Where Kavanagh had once painted Monaghan like a Millet, with a thick and faithful pigment in which men rose from the puddled ground, all wattled in potato mould, he now paints like a Chagall, afloat above his native domain, airborne in the midst of his own dream place rather than earthbound in a literal field. Or perhaps it would be even truer to say that the later regenerated poet in Kavanagh does not paint at all, but draws.

Painting, after all, involves one in a more laboured relationship with a subject – or at least in a more conscious and immersed relationship with a medium – than drawing does. Drawing is closer to the pure moment of perception. The blanknesses which the line travels through in a drawing are not evidence of any incapacity on the artist's part to fill them in. They attest rather to an absolute and all-absorbing need within the line itself to keep on the move. And it is exactly that self-propulsion and airy career of drawing, that mood of buoyancy, that sense of sufficiency in the discovery of a direction rather than any sense of anxiety about the need for a destination, it is this kind of certitude and nonchalance which distinguishes the best of Kavanagh's later work also.

This then is truly creative writing. It does arise from the spontaneous overflow of powerful feelings, but the overflow is not a reactive response to some stimulus in the world out there. Instead, it is a spurt of abundance from a source within and it spills over to irrigate the world beyond the self. This is what Kavanagh is talking about in the poem 'Prelude', when he abjures satire which is a reactive art, an 'unfruitful prayer', and embraces instead the deeper, autonomous and ecstatic art of love itself:

> But satire is unfruitful prayer,
> Only wild shoots of pity there,
> And you must go inland and be
> Lost in compassion's ecstasy,
> Where suffering soars in a summer air –
> The millstone has become a star.

When I read those lines in 1963, I took to their rhythm and was grateful for their skilful way with an octosyllabic metre. But I was too much in love with poetry that painted the world in a thick linguistic pigment to relish fully the line-drawing that was inscribing itself so lightly and freely here. I was still more susceptible to the heavy tarpaulin of the verse of *The Great Hunger* than to the rinsed streamers that fly in the clear subjective breeze of 'Prelude'.

I have learned to value this poetry of inner freedom very highly. It is an example of self-conquest, a style discovered to express this poet's unique response to his universal ordinariness, a way of re-establishing the authenticity of personal experience and surviving as a credible being. So I would now wish to revise a sentence which I wrote ten years ago. I said then that when Kavanagh had consumed the roughage of his Monaghan experience, he ate his heart out. I believe now that it would be truer to say that when he had consumed the roughage of his early Monaghan experience, he had cleared a space where, in Yeats's words, 'The soul recovers radical innocence,/ And learns at last that it is self-delighting,/ Self-appeasing, self-affrighting,/ And that its own sweet will is Heaven's will'. If the price of this learning was too often, in poetic terms, a wilful doggerel, writing which exercised a vindictiveness against the artfulness of art, the rewards of it were a number of poems so full of pure self-possession in the face of death and waste that they prompt that deepest of responses, which the archaic torso of Apollo prompted in Rilke. These poems, with their grievously earned simplicity, make you feel all over again a truth which the mind becomes adept at evading, and which Rilke expressed in a single, simple command: 'You must change your life'.

The Main of Light

E. M. Forster once said that he envisaged *A Passage to India* as a book with a hole in the middle of it. Some poems are like that too. They have openings at their centre which take the reader through and beyond. Shakespeare's Sonnet 60, for example:

> Like as the waves make towards the pebbled shore,
> So do our minutes hasten to their end;
> Each changing place with that which goes before,
> In sequent toil all forwards do contend.
> Nativity, once in the main of light,
> Crawls to maturity, wherewith being crowned,
> Crooked eclipses 'gainst his glory fight,
> And Time that gave doth now his gift confound.

Something visionary happens there in the fifth line. 'Nativity', an abstract noun housed in a wavering body of sound, sets up a warning tremor just before the mind's eye gets dazzled by 'the main of light', and for a split second, we are in the world of the *Paradiso*. The rest of the poem lives melodiously in a world of discourse but it is this unpredictable strike into the realm of pure being that marks the sonnet with Shakespeare's extravagant genius.

In so far as it is a poem alert to the sadness of life's changes but haunted too by a longing for some adjacent 'pure serene', the sonnet rehearses in miniature the whole poignant score of Philip Larkin's poetry. With Larkin, we respond constantly to the melody of intelligence, to a verse that is as much commentary as it is presentation, and it is this encounter between a compassionate, unfoolable mind and its own predicaments – which we are forced to recognize as our predicaments too – that gives his poetry its first appeal. Yet while Larkin is exemplary in the way he sifts the conditions of contemporary life, refuses alibis and pushes consciousness towards an exposed condition that is neither cynicism nor despair, there survives in him a repining for a more crystalline reality to which he might give allegiance. When that repining finds expression, something opens and moments occur which deserve to be called visionary. Because he is suspicious of any easy consolation, he is sparing of such moments, yet when they come they stream into the discursive and exacting world of his poetry with such trustworthy force that they call for attention.

In his introduction to the reissue of *The North Ship*, Larkin recalls a merry and instructive occasion during the period of his infatuation with Yeats. 'I remember Bruce Montgomery snapping, as I droned for the third or fourth time that evening *When such as I cast out remorse, so great a sweetness flows into the breast* . . ., "It's not his job to cast off remorse, but to earn forgiveness." But then Bruce Montgomery had known Charles Williams.' Larkin tells the anecdote to illustrate his early surrender to Yeats's music and also to commend the anti-Romantic, morally sensitive attitude which Montgomery was advocating and which would eventually issue in his conversion to the poetry of Thomas Hardy. Yet it also illustrates that appetite for sweetness flowing into the breast, for the sensation of revelation, which never deserted him. The exchange between Montgomery and himself prefigures the shape of the unsettled quarrel which would be conducted all through the mature poetry, between vision and experience. And if it is that anti-heroic, chastening, humanist voice which is allowed most of the good lines throughout the later poetry, the rebukes it delivers cannot altogether banish the Yeatsian need for a flow of sweetness.

That sweetness flows into the poetry most reliably as a stream of light. In fact, there is something Yeatsian in the way that Larkin, in *High Windows*, places his sun poem immediately opposite and in answer to his moon poem: 'Sad Steps' and 'Solar' face each other on the opened page like the two halves of his poetic personality in dialogue. In 'Sad Steps', the wary intelligence is tempted by a moment of lunar glamour. The renaissance moon of Sir Philip Sidney's sonnet sails close, and the invitation to yield to the 'enormous yes' that love should evoke is potent, even for a man who has just taken a piss:

> I part thick curtains, and am startled by
> The rapid clouds, the moon's cleanliness.
>
> Four o'clock: wedge-shadowed gardens lie
> Under a cavernous, a wind-picked sky.

His vulnerability to desire and hope is transmitted in the Tennysonian cadence of that last line and a half, but immediately the delved brow tightens – 'There's something laughable about this' – only to be tempted again by a dream of fullness, this time in the symbolist transports of language itself – 'O wolves of memory, immensements!' He finally comes out, of course, with a definite, end-stopped 'No'. He refuses to allow the temptations of melody to chloroform the exactions of his common sense. Truth wins over beauty by a few points, and while the appeal of the poem lies in its unconsoled clarity about the seasons of ageing, our nature still tends to run to fill that symbolist hole in the middle.

However, the large yearnings that are kept firmly in their rational place in 'Sad Steps' are given scope to 'climb and return like angels' in 'Solar'. This is frankly a prayer, a hymn to the sun, releasing a generosity that is in no way attenuated when we look twice and find that what is being praised could be as phallic as it is solar. Where the moon is 'preposterous and separate,/ Lozenge of love! Medallion of art!', described in the language of the ironical, emotionally defensive man, the sun is a 'lion face', 'an origin', a 'petalled head of flames', 'unclosing like a hand', all of them phrases of the utmost candid feeling. The poem is unexpected and daring, close to the pulse of primitive poetry, unprotected by any sleight of tone or persona. Here Larkin is bold to stand uncovered in the main of light, far from the hatless one who took off his cycle clips in awkward reverence:

> Coined there among
> Lonely horizontals
> You exist openly.

Our needs hourly
Climb and return like angels.
Unclosing like a hand,
You give forever.

These are the words of someone surprised by 'a hunger in himself to be more serious', although there is nothing in the poem which the happy atheist could not accept. Yet in the 'angels' simile and in the generally choral tone of the whole thing, Larkin opens stops that he usually keeps muted and it is precisely these stops which prove vital to the power and purity of his work.

'Deceptions', for example, depends upon a bright, still centre for its essential poetic power. The image of a window rises to take in the facts of grief, to hold them at bay and in focus. The violated girl's mind lies open 'like a drawer of knives' and most of the first stanza registers the dead-still sensitivity of the gleaming blades and the changing moods of the afternoon light. What we used to consider in our Christian Doctrine classes under the heading of 'the mystery of suffering' becomes actual in the combined sensations of absolute repose and trauma, made substantial in images which draw us into raw identification with the girl:

> The sun's occasional print, the brisk brief
> Worry of wheels along the street outside
> Where bridal London bows the other way,
> And light, unanswerable and tall and wide,
> Forbids the scar to heal, and drives
> Shame out of hiding. All the unhurried day
> Your mind lay open like a drawer of knives.

It is this light-filled dilation at the heart of the poem which transposes it from lament to comprehension and prepares the way for the sharp irony of the concluding lines. I have no doubt that Larkin would have repudiated any suggestion that the beauty of the lines I have quoted is meant to soften the pain, as I have no doubt he would also have repudiated the Pedlar's advice to Wordsworth in 'The Ruined Cottage' where, having told of the long sufferings of Margaret, he bids the poet 'be wise and cheerful'. And yet the Pedlar's advice arises from his apprehension of 'an image of tranquillity' which works in much the same way as the Larkin passage:

> those very plumes,
> Those weeds, and the high spear grass on the wall,
> By mist and silent raindrops silvered o'er.

It is the authenticity of this moment of pacification which to some extent guarantees the Pedlar's optimism; in a similar way the blank tenderness at the heart of Larkin's poem takes it beyond irony and bitterness, though all the while keeping it short of facile consolation: 'I would not dare/ Console you if I could'.

Since Larkin is a poet as explicit as he is evocative, it is no surprise to find him coining terms that exactly describe the kind of effect I am talking about: 'Here', the first poem in *The Whitsun Weddings*, ends by defining it as a sense of 'unfenced existence' and by supplying the experience that underwrites that spacious abstraction:

> Here silence stands
> Like heat. Here leaves unnoticed thicken,
> Hidden weeds flower, neglected waters quicken,
> Luminously-peopled air ascends;
> And past the poppies bluish neutral distance
> Ends the land suddenly beyond a beach
> Of shapes and shingle. Here is unfenced existence:
> Facing the sun, untalkative, out of reach.

It is a conclusion that recalls the conclusion of Joyce's 'The Dead' – and indeed *Dubliners* is a book very close to the spirit of Larkin, whose collected work would fit happily under the title *Englanders*. These concluding lines constitute an epiphany, an escape from the 'scrupulous meanness' of the disillusioned intelligence, and we need only compare 'Here' with 'Show Saturday', another poem that seeks its form by an accumulation of detail, to see how vital to the success of 'Here' is this gesture towards a realm beyond the social and historical. 'Show Saturday' remains encumbered in naturalistic data, and while its conclusion beautifully expresses a nostalgic patriotism which is also an important part of this poet's make-up, the note achieved is less one of plangent vision, more a matter of liturgical wishfulness: 'Let it always be so'.

'If I were called/ To construct a religion/ I should make use of water' – but he could make use of 'Here' as well; and 'Solar'; and 'High Windows'; and 'The Explosion'; and 'Water', the poem from which the lines are taken. It is true that the jaunty tone of these lines, and the downbeat vocabulary later in the poem involving 'sousing,/ A furious devout drench', are indicative of Larkin's unease with the commission he has imagined for himself. But just as 'Solar' and 'Here' yield up occasions where 'unfenced existence' can, without embarrassment to the sceptical man, find space to reveal its pure invitations, so too 'Water' escapes from its man-of-the-world nonchalance into a final stanza which is held like a natural monstrance above the socially defensive idiom of the rest of the poem:

> And I should raise in the east
> A glass of water
> Where any-angled light
> Would congregate endlessly.

The minute light makes its presence felt in Larkin's poetry; he could not resist the romantic poet in himself who must respond with pleasure and alacrity, exclaiming, as it were, 'Already with thee!' The effects are various but they are all extraordinary, from the throwaway surprises of 'a street/ Of blinding windscreens' or 'the differently-swung stars' or 'that high-builded cloud/ Moving at summer's pace', to the soprano delights of this stanza from 'An Arundel Tomb':

> Snow fell, undated. Light
> Each summer thronged the glass. A bright
> Litter of birdcalls strewed the same
> Bone-riddled ground. And up the paths
> The endless altered people came,

– and from that restraint to the manic spasm in this, from 'Livings, II':

[20]

> Guarded by brilliance
> I set plate and spoon,
> And after, divining-cards.
> Lit shelved liners
> Grope like mad worlds westward.

Light, so powerfully associated with joyous affirmation, is even made to serve a ruthlessly geriatric vision of things in 'The Old Fools':

> Perhaps being old is having lighted rooms
> Inside your head, and people in them, acting.

And it is refracted even more unexpectedly at the end of 'High Windows' when one kind of brightness, the brightness of belief in liberation and amelioration, falls from the air which immediately fills with a different, infinitely neutral splendour:

> And immediately

> Rather than words comes the thought of high windows:
> The sun-comprehending glass,
> And beyond it, the deep blue air, that shows
> Nothing, and is nowhere, and is endless.

All these moments spring from the deepest strata of Larkin's poetic self, and they are connected with another kind of mood that pervades his work and which could be called Elysian: I am thinking in particular of poems like 'At Grass', 'MCMXIV', 'How Distant', and most recently, 'The Explosion'. To borrow Geoffrey Hill's borrowing from Coleridge, these are visions of 'the spiritual, Platonic old England', the light in them honeyed by attachment to a dream world that will not be denied because it is at the foundation of the poet's sensibility. It is the light that was on Langland's Malvern, 'in summer season, when soft was the sun', at once local and timeless. In 'The Explosion' the field full of folk has become a coalfield and something Larkin shares with his miners 'breaks ancestrally . . . into/ Regenerate union'.

> The dead go on before us, they
> Are sitting in God's house in comfort,
> We shall see them face to face —

Plain as lettering in the chapels
It was said, and for a second
Wives saw men of the explosion

Larger than in life they managed –
Gold as on a coin, or walking
Somehow from the sun towards them,

One showing the eggs unbroken.

If Philip Larkin had ever composed his version of *The Divine Comedy* he would probably have discovered himself not in a dark wood but a railway tunnel half-way on a journey down England. His inferno proper might have occurred before dawn, as a death-haunted aubade, whence he would emerge into the lighted room inside the head of an old fool, and then his purgatorial ascent would be up through the 'lucent comb' of some hospital building where men in hired boxes would stare out at a wind-tousled sky. We have no doubt about his ability to recount the troubles of such souls who walk the rising ground of 'extinction's alp'. His disillusioned compassion for them has been celebrated and his need to keep numbering their griefs has occasionally drawn forth protests that he narrowed the possibilities of life so much that the whole earth became a hospital. I want to suggest that Larkin also had it in him to write his own version of the *Paradiso*. It might well have amounted to no more than an acknowledgement of the need to imagine 'such attics cleared of me, such absences'; nevertheless, in the poems he has written there is enough reach and longing to show that he did not completely settle for that well-known bargain offer, 'a poetry of lowered sights and patently diminished expectations'.

The Murmur of Malvern

A poet appeases his original needs by learning to make works that seem to be all his own work – Yeats at the stage of *The Wind Among the Reeds*. Then begins a bothersome and exhilarating second need, to go beyond himself and take on the otherness of the world in works that remain his own yet offer rights-of-way to everybody else. This was the kind of understanding and composure Yeats had won by the time he published *The Wild Swans at Coole*, and it is the same kind of authority which Derek Walcott displays in *The Star-Apple Kingdom*.*

'The Schooner Flight', the long poem at the start of the book, is epoch-making. All that Walcott knew in his bones and plied in his thought before this moves like a swell of energy under verse which sails, well rigged and richly cargoed, into the needy future. I imagine he has done for the Caribbean what Synge did for Ireland, found a language woven out of dialect and literature, neither folksy nor condescending, a singular idiom evolved out of one man's inherited divisions and obsessions, an idiom which allows an older life to exult in itself and yet at the same time keeps the cool of 'the new'. A few years ago, in the turbulent and beautiful essay which prefaced his collection of plays, *Dream on Monkey Mountain*, Walcott wrote out of and about the hunger for a proper form, an instrument to bleed off the accumulated humours of his peculiar colonial ague. He has now found that instrument and wields it with rare confidence:

> You ever look up from some lonely beach
> and see a far schooner? Well, when I write

The Star-Apple Kingdom, Farrar, Straus & Giroux, 1979.

this poem, each phrase go be soaked in salt;
I go draw and knot every line as tight
as ropes in this rigging; in simple speech
my common language go be the wind,
my pages the sails of the schooner *Flight*.

The speaker fixes his language in terms that recall Walcott's description of an ideal troupe of actors, 'sinewy, tuned, elated', and the language works for him as a well-disciplined troupe works for the dramatist. It is not for subjective lyric effects but for what James Wright has called 'the poetry of a grown man', one grown to that definitive stage which Yeats called 'the finished man among his enemies'.

For those awakening to the nightmare of history, revenge – Walcott had conceded – can be a kind of vision, yet he himself is not vengeful. Nor is he simply a patient singer of the tears of things. His intelligence is fierce but it is literary. He assumes that art is a power and to be visited by it is to be endangered, but he also knows that works of art endanger nobody else, that they are benign. From the beginning he has never simplified or sold short. Africa and England are in him. The humanist voices of his education and the voices from his home ground keep insisting on their full claims, pulling him in two different directions. He always had the capacity to write with the elegance of a Larkin and make himself a ventriloquist's doll to the English tradition which he inherited, though that of course would have been an attenuation of his gifts, for he also has the capacity to write with the murky voluptuousness of a Neruda and make himself a romantic tongue, indigenous and awash in the prophetic. He did neither, but made a theme of the choice and the impossibility of choosing. And now he has embodied the theme in the person of Shabine, the poor mulatto sailor of the *Flight*, a kind of democratic West Indian Ulysses, his mind full of wind and poetry and women. Indeed, when Walcott lets the sea-breeze freshen in his imagination, the result is a poetry as spacious and heart-lifting as the sea-weather at the opening of Joyce's *Ulysses*, a poetry that comes from no easy evocation of mood but from stored sensations of the actual:

In idle August, while the sea soft,
and leaves of brown islands stick to the rim
of this Caribbean, I blow out the light
by the dreamless face of Maria Concepcion
to ship as a seaman on the schooner *Flight*.
Out in the yard turning gray in the dawn,
I stood like a stone and nothing else move
but the cold sea rippling like galvanize
and the nail holes of stars in the sky roof,
till a wind start to interfere with the trees.

It is a sign of Walcott's mastery that his fidelity to West Indian speech now leads him not away from but right into the genius of English. When he wrote these opening lines, how conscious was he of another morning departure, another allegorical early-riser? The murmur of Malvern is under that writing, for surely it returns to an origin in *Piers Plowman*:

In summer season, when soft was the sun,
I rigged myself up in a long robe, rough like a sheep's,
With skirts hanging like a hermit's, unholy of works,
Went wide in this world, wonders to hear.
But on a May morning, on Malvern Hills,
A marvel befell me – magic it seemed.
I was weary of wandering and went for a rest
Under a broad bank, by a brook's side;
And as I lay lolling, looking at the water,
I slid into a sleep . . .

The whole passage could stand as an epigraph to Walcott's book in so far as it is at once speech and melody, amorous of the landscape, matter-of-fact but capable of modulation to the visionary. Walcott's glamorous, voluble Caribbean harbours recall Langland's field full of folk. Love and anger inspire both writers, and both manage – in Eliot's phrase – to fuse the most ancient and most civilized mentality. The best poems in *The Star-Apple Kingdom* are dream visions; the high moments are hallucinatory, cathartic, redemptive even. Here, for example, is a passage from 'Koenig of the River', where Koenig appears on his shallop like some Dantesque shade arisen out of the imperial dream, being forced to relive it in order to comprehend it:

> Around the bend the river poured its silver
> like some remorseful mine, giving and giving
> everything green and white: white sky, white
> water, and the dull green like a drumbeat
> of the slow-sliding forest, the green heat;
> then, on some sandbar, a mirage ahead:
> fabric of muslin sails, spider-web rigging,
> a schooner, foundered on black river mud,
> was rising slowly up from the riverbed,
> and a top-hatted native reading an inverted
> newspaper.
>   'Where's our Queen?' Koenig shouted.
> 'Where's our Kaiser?'
>   The nigger disappeared.
> Koenig felt that he himself was being read
> like the newspaper or a hundred-year-old novel.

There is a magnificence and pride about this art – specifically the art, not specially the politics – that rebukes that old British notion of 'Commonwealth literature': Walcott possesses English more deeply and sonorously than most of the English themselves. I can think of nobody now writing with more imperious linguistic gifts. And in spite of the sheen off those lines, I suspect he is not so much interested in the 'finish' of his work as in its drive. He has written lyrics of memorable grace – 'In a Green Night' and 'Coral' come to mind as two different kinds of excellence – and his deliberately designed early sonnet sequence 'Tales of the Islands' guaranteed the possibility of these latest monologues and narratives. His work for the stage has paid into his address to the poetry until the latter now moves itself and us in a thoroughly dramatic way. 'The Star-Apple Kingdom', for example, is a discursive and meditative poem, a dive into the cultural and political matter of post-colonial Jamaica, yet the pitch of the writing could hardly be described as either meditative or discursive. Again, there is a dream-heavy thing at work, as if the years of analysis and commitment to thinking justly had resolved themselves for the poet into a sound half-way between sobbing and sighing. The poem does not have the pure windfall grace of 'The Schooner Flight' – in places it sags into 'writing' – but its pitch and boldness make a lovely orchestration of the music of ocean and the music of history:

> What was the Caribbean? A green pond mantling
> behind the Great House columns of Whitehall,
> behind the Greek façades of Washington,
> with bloated frogs squatting on lily pads
> like islands, islands that coupled sadly as turtles
> engendering islets, as the turtle of Cuba
> mounting Jamaica engendered the Caymans, as, behind
> the hammerhead turtle of Haiti–San Domingo
> trailed the little turtles from Tortuga to Tobago;
> he followed the bobbing trek of the turtles
> leaving America for the open Atlantic,
> felt his own flesh loaded like the pregnant beaches
> with their moon-guarded eggs – they yearned for
> Africa . . .

Walcott's poetry has passed the stage of self-questioning, self-exposure, self-healing, to become a common resource. He is no propagandist. What he would propagate is magnanimity and courage and I am sure that he would agree with Hopkins's affirmation that feeling, and in particular love, is the great power and spring of verse. This book is awash with love of people and places and language: love as knowledge, love as longing, love as consummation, at one time the Sermon on the Mount, at another *Antony and Cleopatra*:

> He lies like a copper palm
> tree at three in the afternoon
> by a hot sea
> and a river, in Egypt, Tobago.
>
> Her salt marsh dries in the heat
> where he foundered
> without armour.
> He exchanged an empire for her beads of sweat,

[27]

the uproar of arenas,
the changing surf
of senators, for
this ceiling over silent sand –

this grizzled bear, whose fur,
moulting, is silvered –
for this quick fox with her
sweet stench.

('Egypt, Tobago')

There is something risky about such large appropriations, but they are legitimate because Walcott's Caribbean and Cleopatra's Nile have the same sweltering awareness of the cynicism and brutality of political adventures. He is not going beyond the field of his own imagery; he is appropriating Shakespeare, not expropriating him – the unkindest post-colonial cut of all.

Conscious-maker that he is, Derek Walcott is certainly aware that when the whirligig of time brings in such revenges, they turn out to be more ironies than revenges. His sense of options and traditions is highly developed and his deliberate progress as a writer has not ended. Much that he inherited as inchoate communal plight has been voiced, especially in the dramatic modes of this volume, yet I am not sure that he won't return inwards to the self, to refine the rhetoric. 'Forest of Europe', the poem dedicated to Joseph Brodsky, is aimed at the centre of Walcott's themes – language, exile, art – and is written with the surge of ambition that marks him as a major voice. But I feel that the wilful intelligence has got too much of the upper hand in the poem, that the thrill of addressing a heroic comrade in the art has forced the note. I rejoice in everything the poem says – 'what's poetry, if it is worth its salt/but a phrase men can pass from hand to mouth?' – yet the poem is not securely in possession of its tone. Which could never be said of Shabine, who deals with the big themes in his own nonchalant way:

I met History once, but he ain't recognize me,
a parchment Creole, with warts
like an old sea bottle, crawling like a crab
through the holes of shadow cast by the net

of a grille balcony; cream linen, cream hat.
I confront him and shout, 'Sir, is Shabine!
They say I'se your grandson. You remember Grandma,
your black cook, at all?' The bitch hawk and spat.
A spit like that worth any number of words.
But that's all them bastards have left us: words.

The Poems of the Dispossessed Repossessed

My first sense of the literary tradition in Irish was a dark green cliff of books looming over me as I knelt like some latter-day croppy boy murmuring 'Bless me, Father . . .' Confessions in St Columb's College were held in the priest's rooms on Saturday nights – after the showers – and the bookcases of my confessor were packed with a complete range of the Early Irish Texts Society's publications. It all came back to me as I read *An Duanaire;** but I was also suddenly aware how much of my sense of the tradition had remained a sentiment rather than a possession acquired 'by great labour'.

Significant work done in Irish between 1600 and 1900 is here edited by Seán Ó Tuama and translated by Thomas Kinsella in such a way that it has something to say about the direction Irish poetry should take, now and in the future. For example, it would heal the hidden fault in that very phrase 'Irish poetry', by closing the rift between the Irish language past and the English language present. *An Duanaire* implies a community of feeling between us and our forebears and could carry as an epigraph Nadezhda Mandelstam's stirring definition: 'A real community is unshakeable, indubitable, and enduring . . . It remains unaffected and whole even when the people united by it are already in their graves.'

There are two ways with anthologies: Palgrave's, and (though he was not strictly speaking an anthologist) Pound's. Palgrave's way involves culling the beauties, orphaning them

* *An Duanaire 1600–1900: Poems of the Dispossessed.* Dánta Gaeilge curtha i lathair ag Seán Ó Tuama, with verse translations by Thomas Kinsella, Dolmen Press, 1981.

from their context and presenting them for our admiration as occasions of pleasure. The anthologist retires, his taste is present mostly as a confirmation of current notions of 'good taste'. Pound's way is the opposite: the anthologist is more pedagogue than connoisseur, his taste is personal and often counter-cultural; he is concerned to establish contexts and to have his choice of poems read not just as isolated lyric moments but as the plot of a whole imaginative action. Palgrave's way is the commoner one, and just as well, because it takes a gifted poetic and historical intelligence to enter upon the other way. But Ó Tuama and Kinsella are splendidly equipped for it and have gone at their task with deliberate intent. The anthology is educative, historically sensitive and designed to be representative of a whole Irish continuum in which public events and private ways of feeling have nourished each other.

What distinguishes this parallel text from the ones in the old green and gold tomes of the Early Irish Texts Society is that this one aims for critical discrimination rather than scholarly inclusiveness. The editors are not establishing a canon but defining a sensibility and an achievement. What distinguishes it again from collections of translations such as Lord Longford's and Frank O'Connor's is that the translations here are not asking to be taken as alternatives to the originals but are offered as paths to lead our eyes left across the page, back to the Irish. There is an ideal of service behind it all, a literary ideal, it should be stressed, not a propagandist one: we are led to the Irish poems not in order to warm ourselves at the racial embers but to encounter works of art that belong to world literature.

Part of Seán Ó Tuama's contribution to our critical perspectives has been to establish links between the tradition of poetry in Irish and the medieval *amour courtois* convention in Europe. He would remind us that the *Langue d'oc* is part of the *langue* of *is agus tá*. His scholarship is matched only by his insouciance and he is consequently less hung up than, say, Corkery was about Irish poetry *vis-à-vis* English poetry. His Renaissance is Mediterranean, full of sunlight and vernacular energy, not the black-capped, Latin-lipped one which stares out of Holbein. I can imagine him, for example, linking Ó Rathaille's pride with Dante's, pointing up their common bitterness and loss, their sense of exile from the first good world, and indeed it is salutary to be able to conceive of Ó Rathaille's rawness of feeling, his partisan fury and his bare-handed single combat with the ruin of his times as a pattern of poetic fate and not entirely an aberration and deprivation. Too often the tradition of English poetry – especially contemporary seventeenth- and eighteenth-century poetry in England, with its bookish clergymen and witty lords – forces itself into the mind as the norm against which everything is measured.

There is no danger of Thomas Kinsella pulling against his colleague here. He too has been concerned to widen the lens, to make Irish poetry in English get out from under the twilight shades of the specifically English tradition. In his own work he has long since – and deliberately – given up considerations of 'the reader's comfort'. He has strenuously punished the lyricist in himself who carried off such stylish performances in the early books. As the influence of Pound and indeed of Ó Rathaille has taken hold, he has gradually evicted traces of Audenesque, iambic – strictly English – melody, in order to find a denser, more laconic, more indigenous way with the poetic line. When I say 'indigenous' I do not mean the alternative charm of some kind of 'Irish note' but rather something genetic at the roots of Kinsella's own Dublin speech. In fact, the rhythms of Joyce's prose are finally more relevant to his endeavour than the metrics and assonances of the native tradition.

So the refusal of rhyme and the disdain of a charming tune which informs these translations is all of a piece with the sterner procedures of Kinsella's later work. And indeed the unrepentant note which he appended to 'Butcher's Dozen' in his recent collection, *Fifteen Dead*, is continuous with the swell of political energy in the poems of the middle section of this anthology. Much of the work of Ó Bruadair, Ó Rathaille, Seán Clárach MacDomhnaill and others has the same rage and certitude as Kinsella's own Bloody Sunday poem. Moreover, the English version of this book's title, 'Poems of the Dispossessed', explicitly brings it into line between the political sourness of poetry in Irish after the Battle of Kinsale and other work in English by the translator which is tinged with similar disappointment and disaffection. In other words, in spite of his celebrated assertion about the fractured nature of the Irish literary tradition, Kinsella's involvement in this new enterprise of repossession attests to his trust in the continuing efficacy of that tradition. His advocacy of Pearse as a translator, for example, is based on thoroughly literary criteria – fidelity to the originals, lack of interference with the texts – yet one senses that Kinsella would see this integrity as the natural concomitant of Pearse's extreme, uncompromised, and by now unfashionable political ideals.

As a translator, Kinsella is most interested in tone, to try to carry the tone of Irish across the linguistic divide. Tone is the inner life of a language, a secret spirit at play behind or at odds with what is being said and how it is being structured in syntax and figures of speech. It has subtly to do with the deepest value system that the group speaking the language is possessed by. In another context, for example, Seán Ó Tuama has suggested that the goliardic strain in medieval continental poetry, the ironical and mocking intelligence of it, appealed immediately to the Irish spirit which did not take altogether naturally to the aureate philosophical apparatus of *amour courtois* proper. There was, if you like, a tone to the goliardic verse which the Irish recognized, picked up and made their own – and Kinsella, by implication, would like the coherence and astringency of the Irish tone to penetrate and alloy our own literary English. Hence the value which the introduction places upon the dramatic or storytelling voice as opposed to any resourcefulness of image and metaphor, and hence also to praise of a 'bluntness of attitude' in the accentual poetry of the seventeenth and eighteenth centuries.

What this means in practice can be seen by a couple of comparisons. The third stanza of Poem 2 in *An Duanaire* goes:

> *I dteampal ná i mainistir,*
> *cé madh reilig nó réadmhagh,*
> *dá bhfaice ná dá bhfaicear-sa*
> *ná féach orm is ní fhéachfad.*

The first half of the stanza is like a stone wall of nouns, the consonantal blocks of the first line loosening to a gravelly mouthful of vowels in the second line; and then the verbs take over as the reflexive play of sense and sound becomes at once more throwaway and more calculated. Lord Longford put it into English like this:

> And if we meet, as we may do,
>   At church or on the plain,
> You'll pass me by as I will you
>   Nor turn your head again.

This is dainty and tripping, closer to the Ballymena Girls' Choir singing 'Kitty of Coleraine' than to the cool anatomy of a passion. It has its own felicitous movement but it does lead away from the music of the original, and the word 'plain', for example, is subtly wrong for an Irish countryside of chapel and graveyard. Kinsella keeps the nouns where the nouns were and the verbs where the verbs were, keeps closer to a speaking voice than to a flouncing lyric one, is terser, less comfortable.

> In the chapel, in the abbey,
>   the churchyard or the open air,
> if we two should chance to meet,
>   don't look, and I won't look at you.

Of course, to be faithful to word-order and directness of utterance he sacrifices rhyme, and in this case as in many others the sacrifice is well worth it. There is a steadfastness about the whole procedure, and the word 'steadfast' itself which starts up boldly in the first line of Kinsella's 'Lament for Art O'Laoghaire' seems etymologically apt for his achievement. The word is charged with ideas of foundation and place – 'stead' – and fidelity and perseverance – 'fast'. O'Connor gave 'my love and my delight' for 'mo ghrá go daingean thú'; Kinsella has 'my steadfast love', which is perfect.

Yet in spite of the literary morality that made him buckle down to sense and tone, I do regret Kinsella's shunning of rhyme and melody. Poetry in Irish is happily alive with both, with all kinds of verbal philandering and showing-off, and the man who wrote 'A Lady of Quality' and 'Downstream' is not entirely immune to the appeal of all that. Indeed he can still surrender to the delicacy of it with very poignant results, as in his version of 'Ag Chríost an síol':

To Christ the seed, to Christ the crop,
in barn of Christ may we be brought.

To Christ the sea, to Christ the fish,
in nets of Christ may we be caught.

The original has 'iothlainn Dé' in line two and 'líonta Dé' in line four, but to repeat 'Christ' rather than introduce 'God' in the English is the proper and enlivening touch here. A venial sin against fidelity becomes an actual grace for the poetry in English. And even in his most penitentially literal mood, should he have gone through with 'much angered at me are all my people, and my love far off'? The strength of this is that when we cast eyes left we come home to 'tá mo mhuintir go mór i bhfeirg liom is mo ghrá i bhfad uaim'. Its weakness is that on its own it sails near to Myles na gCopaleen parody. Yet it is precisely the integrity of Kinsella's method all through this substantial book which brings him to these dangerous straits: to appreciate the difference between his freedom as a creative poet and his obedience as a translator we need only compare the *Duanaire* version of 'Is fada liom oíche fhírfliuch' and his poem 'The Poet Aodhagán Ó Rathaille Homesick in Old Age' in *Nightwalker*.

An Duanaire is a re-education in our poetry, a recuperative event. The range is great, in time and substance, from the terrific jealousy poems of the seventeenth century to the tender folk poetry at the end of the book. The great aislings and laments of Munster, the melodies of MacCuarta and MacCumthaigh from Ulster, the big love songs of Connacht, the epigrams of Haicéad, the elegance and toughness of Feiritéar, the hammer-and-tongs of Merriman – to those of us who have been shy to lay claim to it all because of our lack of certainty about understanding it, Seán Ó Tuama and Thomas Kinsella have given a book of great worth and importance, one that could mark an epoch.

The Impact of Translation

Here, to begin with, is a poem by Czeslaw Milosz, translated by
the author and Robert Pinsky, which Robert Pinsky read to me
some years ago at his home in Berkeley:

INCANTATION

Human reason is beautiful and invincible.
No bars, no barbed wire, no pulping of books,
No sentence of banishment can prevail against it.
It establishes the universal ideas in language,
And guides our hand so we write Truth and Justice
With capital letters, lie and oppression with small.
It puts what should be above things as they are,
Is an enemy of despair and a friend of hope.
It does not know Jew from Greek or slave from master,
Giving us the estate of the world to manage.
It saves austere and transparent phrases
From the filthy discord of tortured words.
It says that everything is new under the sun,
Opens the congealed fist of the past.
Beautiful and very young are Philo-Sophia
And poetry, her ally in the service of the good.
As late as yesterday Nature celebrated their birth,
The news was brought to the mountains by a unicorn and an
    echo.
Their friendship will be glorious, their time has no limit.
Their enemies have delivered themselves to destruction.

My first experience of these lines, spoken in the upstairs study
of a silent house, empty that afternoon except for ourselves,

[36]

was altogether thrilling. There is always a slight element of the conspiratorial present when a poem is read aloud between two people, a sense of a private march being stolen, perhaps, too, a sense of a risk being taken, since the other party may find the whole performance a little jejune. In this case, moreover, the feeling of collusion was made all the stronger for me because we were enjoying a poem which did things forbidden within an old dispensation to which I was admittedly more subject than my host, who had once studied with Yvor Winters. The poem was, for example, full of abstractions, and to a member of the generation whose poetic ABCs included 'A Few Don'ts for Imagists', these unabashed abstract nouns and conceptually aerated adjectives should have been altogether out of the question. 'Glorious', 'beautiful', 'universal', 'banishment', 'despair', 'discord', 'destruction' – usually one would have demurred at the torpor of this vocabulary, its indifference to the expectation of particularity. Usually, too, orthodox assumptions would have been ruffled by the unembarrassed didacticism of the lines. Nothing was being dramatized; the speaker in the poem seemed to be irrefutably one with the voice of the poet; he seemed, moreover, to know exactly what he wanted to say before he began to say it, and indeed the poem aspired to deliver what we had once long ago been assured it was not any poem's business to deliver: a message. It proclaimed in argent speech truths we had assumed to be previous to poetry, so richly established outside its formal citadel that they could never be admitted undisguised or untransmuted through the eye of the lyric needle. Now here they were in a modern poem – big, pulpit-worthy affirmations, boosted all the further by that one metaphorical flight about a unicorn and an echo in the mountains, and fortified by the hovering irony of the final line.

What was going on? The crucial point was, of course, the title, 'Incantation'. This is a spell, uttered to bring about a desirable state of affairs, rather than a declaration that such a state of affairs truly exists – for nobody knows better than the author how long and how invincibly the enemies of human reason can prevail. What gives the poem its ultimate force is, therefore, the intense loss we recognize behind its proclamation of trust. And given that the true subject is loss, should it matter, then, who composed it? Is it not sufficient that rhythm and diction and tone be effectively bonded?

That very bonding, however, is effected in great part by our awareness of the context from which Czeslaw Milosz's text emerges. It counted for much that this poem was written by somebody who had resisted the Nazi occupation of Poland and had broken from the ranks of the People's Republic after the war and paid for the principle and pain of all that with a lifetime of exile and self-scrutiny. The poem, in fact, is a bonus accruing to a life lived in the aftermath of right and hurtful decisions, and it elicits the admiration of English-speaking readers partly because of this extra-literary consideration. It is therefore typical of work by many other poets, particularly in the Soviet republics and the Warsaw Pact countries, whose poetry not only witnesses the poet's refusal to lose his or her cultural memory but also testifies thereby to the continuing efficacy of poetry itself as a necessary and fundamental human act.

What translation has done over the last couple of decades is not only to introduce us to new literary traditions but also to link the new literary experience to a modern martyrology, a record of courage and sacrifice which elicits our unstinted admiration. So, subtly, with a kind of hangdog intimation of desertion, poets in English have felt compelled to turn their gaze East and have been encouraged to concede that the locus of greatness is shifting away from their language. This is not to suggest that poets and readers are not still sensible of the achievements of Yeats, Frost, Pound, Eliot, Auden and all the rest as the unlooked-for events in poetry which they were and are – geological occurrences which have altered the contours of the language we look back upon. These remain undeniable forms in our literary memory. Yet gradually, wraiths from beyond have begun to move in the Elysian background. We have been made conscious, for example, of the passionate spirits of Russian poetry in the teens, twenties and thirties of this century. Whether we can truly know the driven brilliance of their work through translation is not a question I wish to address here. It seems self-evident that what the reader who does not speak Russian experiences as the poem in translation is radically and logically different from what the native speaker experiences, phonetics and feelings being so intimately related in the human make-up. What I am suggesting, rather, is that our sense of the fate and scope of modern Russian poetry has implicitly established a bench at which subsequent work will have to justify itself. How often, in epigraphs to essays and poems, or as the subject of essays and poems, or as corroborating allusions in essays and poems, do we not nowadays come upon the names of Tsvetaeva and Akhmatova and the Mandelstams and Pasternak? These, and many others – Gumilev, Esenin, Mayakovsky – have become heroic names. They are the ones who toed the line, not just the verse line but the line where courage is tested, where to stand by what you write is to have to stand your ground and take the consequences. For these poets, the mood of writing is the indicative mood and for that reason they constitute a shadow-challenge to poets who dwell in the conditional, the indeterminate mood which has grown characteristic of so much of the poetry one has grown used to reading in the journals and new books, particularly in the United States.

Yet in the case of the heroes, it is not so much their procedures on the page which are influential as the composite image which has been projected of their conduct. That image, congruent with the reality, features a poet tested by dangerous times. What is demanded is not any great public act of confrontation or submission, but rather a certain self-censorship, an agreement to forge, in the bad sense, the uncreated conscience of a race. Their resistance to this pressure is not initially or intentionally political, but there is of course a spin-off, a ripple effect, to their deviant artistic conduct. It is the refusal by this rearguard minority which exposes to the majority the abjectness of their collapse, as they flee for security into whatever self-deceptions the party line requires of them. And it is because they effect this exposure that the poets become endangered: people are never grateful for being reminded of their moral cowardice.

In the professionalized literary milieu of the West, the poet is susceptible to self-deprecation and scepticism. The poet in the United States, for example, is aware that the machine of reputation-making and book distribution, whether it elevates or ignores him or her, is indifferent to the moral and ethical force of the poetry being distributed. A grant-aided pluralism of fashions and schools, a highly amplified language of praise which becomes the language of promotion and marketing – all this which produces from among the most gifted a procession of ironists and dandies and reflexive talents, produces also a subliminal awareness of the alternative conditions and an anxious over-the-shoulder glance toward them.

All the same, poets in the West do not regard their colleagues under pressure in the simple-minded spirit sometimes attributed to them, which is a caricature of their subtler complexes. Western poets do not assume that a tyrannical situation is mitigated because it produces heroic artists and last-ditch art. They do not in any way envy the hard fate of the artist but rather admire the faith in art itself which becomes manifest in the extreme conditions. They stand in awe as life rises to the climactic and on the whole aesthetic state which Yeats imagined as 'Black out; Heaven blazing into the head:/ Tragedy wrought to its uttermost'.

Many contemporaries writing in English have been displaced from an old at-homeness in their mother tongue and its hitherto world-defining poetic heritage. I am all the more persuaded of this when a talented young British poet brings out a volume written in the voice of an apocryphal Eastern European poet and which therefore, necessarily, masquerades as a translation. Christopher Reid, author of *Katerina Brac* (1985), had been classed until its publication as one of those English poets dubbed 'Martians' after Craig Raine's eponymous 'A Martian Sends a Postcard Home'. Reid was and remains an adept of this school of writing, a mode involving a defamiliarization, a sleight-of-image process by which one thing is seen in terms of another thing; but I believe it is symptomatic that Reid's escape from such a patented idiom should be by way of echoing certain poetic noises he could not naturally achieve in his own voice.

I am reminded of Stephen Dedalus's enigmatic declaration that the shortest way to Tara was via Holyhead, implying that departure from Ireland and inspection of the country from the outside was the surest way of getting to the core of Irish experience. Might we not nowadays affirm, analogously, that the shortest way to Whitby, the monastery where Caedmon sang the first Anglo-Saxon verses, is via Warsaw and Prague? To put it more directly, contemporary English poetry has become aware of the insular and eccentric nature of English experience in all the literal and extended meanings of those adjectives. England's island status, its off-centre European positioning, its history of non-defeat and non-invasion since 1066, these enviable and (as far as the English are concerned) normative conditions have ensured a protracted life within the English psyche for the assumption that a possible and desirable congruence exists between domestic and imagined reality. But Christopher Reid's book represents a moment of doubt; and it represents also the delayed promise, though not the complete fulfilment, of a native British modernism.

This was potentially present in the stylistic intensities and the dislocated geopolitical phantasmagorias of early Auden, and in the visionary, if low-wattage poetry of Edwin Muir. Muir's two post-war volumes, *The Labyrinth* in 1949 and *One Foot in Eden* in 1956, are not like anything that was going on just then on the poetic home front. These books showed no signs of being influenced either by the neo-Romantic rhetoric of George Barker and Dylan Thomas or the tight formation-flying of the Empson/Auden division. It so happened that it was the Movement poets, Larkin, Davie, Enright and others, the inheritors in the Empson/Auden line, who pointed the way for much of what happened over the next twenty years. Yet it could be thought a matter of regret that Edwin Muir – the poet who translated Kafka in the 1920s and who witnessed the Communist takeover in Czechoslovakia after the war, the one poet from the British island with an eschatological if somewhat somnambulistic address to the historical moment in post-war Europe – did not succeed better in bringing the insular/vernacular/British imagination into more traumatic contact with a reality of which *Katerina Brac* is the wistful and literary after-image. Here, for example, is Muir's 'The Interrogation', from *The Labyrinth*:

> We could have crossed the road but hesitated,
> And then came the patrol;
> The leader conscientious and intent,

The men surly, indifferent.
While we stood by and waited
The interrogation began. He says the whole
Must come out now, who, what we are,
Where we have come from, with what purpose, whose
Country or camp we fight for or betray.
Question on question.
We have stood and answered through the standing day
And watched across the road beyond the hedge
The careless lovers in pairs go by,
Hand linked in hand, wandering another star,
So near we could shout to them. We cannot choose
Answer or action here,
Though still the careless lovers saunter by
And the thoughtless field is near.
We are on the very edge,
Endurance almost done,
And still the interrogation is going on.

There is something different here, in spite of some quite specific Auden echoes. 'The Interrogation' anticipates by a couple of decades the note which would be heard when A. Alvarez began to edit his influential Penguin Modern European Poets series in the late 1960s, a note as knowledgeable as it was powerless to survive with any sort of optimism in the light of what it knew.

So Muir's poem is 'European' – but in a way very different from the way that Robert Lowell's *Imitations* is 'European'. Those translations, which appeared a dozen years later, were still confident in their cultural and historical self-possession. Lowell's versions of canonical poems from the Greek, Latin, Italian, French, German and Russian were offered as bridges to link up with an undemolished past. The breach made by the war years did not succeed in dissociating Lowell and his contemporaries living under the roof of English from the enterprise of the great modernists. Pound and Eliot and Joyce may have regarded themselves as demolitionists of sorts but from a later perspective they turned out to be conservationists, keeping open lines to the classical inheritance of European literature. In getting ready for the end of a world, they extended its life expectancy indefinitely.

If, therefore, Lowell, Randall Jarrell, Keith Douglas, Louis MacNeice, Louis Simpson, Dylan Thomas, and Eliot himself all testified at different moments and in different registers in their poetry to the horror and fury of the war, they did so with an unbroken historical nerve. The war may have made as great a gap in their sense of human nature as bombs made in cities, but the poetic tradition inside which they worked cushioned the blast. It was as if a kind of cultural air-raid shelter was prepared by Eliot's reinforcement of the idea of tradition itself. I hope I will not be considered a boor or an ingrate if I adduce the famous passage in 'Little Gidding' as an illustration of how effective the beauties of the poetic heritage could be in keeping at bay the actual savagery of the wartime experience. There, in the Dantesque set-piece of the dawn patrol, Hitler's Luftwaffe could be sent packing as a dark dove beneath the horizon of its homing, and the All Clear after an air raid could recompose the morning by recourse to matutinal airs which had once drifted from the dew of a high eastern hill towards the battlements of Elsinore.

In 'Little Gidding', as Eliot's persona wanders through the newsreel familiarity of a blitz, he constitutes a proof – sufficient for the imagination, at least – that an ordained and suprahistorical reality persists, and it is one of the triumphs of the poem to make such a faith provisionally tenable. But it is Muir's persona, in 'The Interrogation', who seems to be more truly our representative, stunned and ineffective at the centre of a menacing pageant – what Eliot called the vast panorama of violence and futility which is contemporary history. If Muir's poetry is far less authoritative and ungainsayable than Eliot's, there is nevertheless audible in it a note which sounds both elegiac for and posthumous to the European civilization which produced it. We who live and have our being in English know that this note is proper to the world we have come to inhabit, to the extent that our own recent history of consumerist freedom and eerie nuclear security seems less authentic to us than the tragically tested lives of those who live beyond the pale of all this fiddle. Which is why the note sounded by translated poetry from that world beyond – pitched intently and in spite of occupation, holocaust, concentration camps and the whole apparatus of totalitarianism – is so credible, desolating, and resuscitative.

I would propose, then, that there was a road not taken in poetry in English in this century, a road travelled once by the young Auden and the middle-aged Muir. Further, because we have not lived the tragic scenario which such imaginations presented to us as the life appropriate to our times, our capacity to make a complete act of faith in our vernacular poetic possessions has been undermined. Consequently, we are all the more susceptible to translations which arrive like messages from those holding their own much, much further down the road not taken by us – because, happily, it was a road not open to us. When we read translations of the poets of Russia and Eastern Europe, 'We are on the very edge . . . And still the interrogation is going on.'

The Fully Exposed Poem

In spite of a period of castigation about the necessity for 'intelligence' and 'irony', poetry in English has not moved all that far from the shelter of the Romantic tradition. Even our self-mocking dandies pirouette to a narcotic music. The dream's the thing, not the diagnosis. Inwardness, yearnings and mergings of the self towards nature, cadences that drink at spots of time – in general the hopes of poets and readers still realize themselves within contexts like these. We still expect the poetic imagination to be sympathetic rather than analytic. 'Intellect' still tends to summon its rhyme from Wordsworth's pejorative 'dissect'.

I presume, however, that *Sagittal Section*, the earlier of these two books by Miroslav Holub,* is a title which inclines positively towards the knife of intellect, although it is interesting that 'sagittal section' was a phrase not to be found in my OED; instead there was 'sagittal suture', as if the English language itself was working against the Czech poet's endeavour, preferring ideas of knitting and junction to those of splitting and cutting. At any rate, the given phrase meant 'the median antero-posterior suture between the two parietal bones on the vertex of the skull', so a sagittal section – and the cover illustration of a bisected skull enforces this – involved opening up what is closed at this line, a surgical inspection, a scientific point of view. This is hardly surprising, considering that Holub is chief research immunologist at the Institute for Clinical and

* *Sagittal Section: Poems New and Selected*, translated by Stuart Friebert and Dana Hábová, FIELD Translation Series 3, 1980; *Interferon or On Theater*, translated by David Young and Dana Hábová, FIELD Translation Series 7, 1982.

Experimental Medicine in Prague and, as Leslie Thomas observes in his Introduction, Holub the poet and Holub the scientist both share a 'professional attitude'.

It should be said right away that the book delivers what the title promises – a laying bare of things, not so much the skull beneath the skin, more the brain beneath the skull; the shape of relationships, politics, history; the rhythms of affection and disaffection; the ebb and flow of faith, hope, violence, art. It is a very nimble and very serious anatomy of the world, too compassionate to be vindictive, too sceptical to be entranced, a poetry in which intelligence and irony make their presence felt without displacing delight and the less acerbic wisdoms.

Although this is Miroslav Holub's first book to be published in the United States, many people will know the work already from the Penguin selection published in London in 1967, translated by Ian Milner and George Theiner. Since then, two more of his books have appeared in England and his name is now confidently and properly invoked by people in search of those exemplary poets who vindicate the *utile* dimensions of their art without betraying their obligations to the *dulce*. There is something tremendously capable and good-humoured about the work, a high-spirited distrust. It has in it all the worn-down truth-to-life of the disillusioned man, but it also has a contrary and heartening vision of a possible good based upon optimism about decencies and impulses in the usual life. It is at once down-to-earth and wide open. At the moment when it reduces things to their plainest and baldest dimensions, it can offer a sense of release and a new scope:

> The Earth is turning,
>   says the pupil.
> No, the Earth is turning,
>   says the teacher.
>
> Thy leaf has perish'd in the green,
>   says the pupil.
> No, Thy leaf has perish'd in the green,
>   says the teacher.
>
> Two and two is four,
>   says the pupil.

Two and two is four,
  the teacher corrects him.

Because the teacher knows better.
                    ('Teacher')

This is neither tricksy nor outraged. There is no relish in
Holub's exposure, more a concern that the true shape of things
should be common knowledge. In some of his most approachable poems it is as if he is just checking the reader's equipment
for survival, ticking off a list of unspoken truths but taking no
credit for having the full list naturally at his disposal. I believe
him when he says

  I like writing for people untouched by poetry; for instance,
  for those who do not even know that it should at all be for
  them. I would like them to read poems as naturally as they
  read the papers, or go to a football game.

But notwithstanding this democratic robustness, there is
nothing cut-price about the goods on offer, no courtship of the
lowest common denominator, no corny sympathy for the likes
of 'The Corporal Who Killed Archimedes':

          With one bold stroke
          he killed the circle, tangent
          and point of intersection
          in infinity.

          On penalty
          of quartering
          he banned numbers
          from three up.

          Now in Syracuse
          he leads a school of philosophers,
          for another thousand years
          squats on his halberd
          and writes:

          one   two
          one   two

one   two
one   two

For all their persuasive anecdotal elegance, the poems quoted here are just a beginning, a way in. Holub's laconic accuracies do indeed express themselves happily in such diagrams of history and politics, in what has been called an 'Aesopic' language, but there is in the work as well an inventive, sportive lyricism which can engage the more poignant registers in our make-up, yet which disallows us any savouring of our own pathos. The poem that opens this selection, for example, is both merry and profound, as immediately winning as a strip cartoon and at the same time Olympian in its long view of human aggression and human need. It offers aesthetic satisfactions that are fully Keatsian – it surprises by a fine excess, the imagery rises and sets, it strikes us as a remembrance – yet we sense that its fullness and aesthetic repose are not enough for the writer. Under his tolerance for man's behaviour there abides a need to judge, to balance lament and rebuke. In spite of the justice and largeness of the vision, in spite of the accommodation arrived at with things as they are, something unnerving, a recognition of the deplorable, swims in the wake of the poem and refuses to allow us to get away with taking it simply as 'the words on the page'.

> Someone
> just climbed to the top of the cliffs
> and began to curse the sea.
>
> Dumb water, stupid pregnant water,
> slow, slimy copy of the sky,
> you peddler between sun and moon,
> pettifogging pawnbroker of shells,
> soluble, loud-mouthed bull,
> fertilizing the rocks with your blood,
> suicidal sword
> dashed to bits on the headland,
> hydra, hydrolizing the night,
> breathing salty clouds of silence,
> spreading jelly wings

in vain, in vain,
gorgon, devouring its own body,

water, you absurd flat skull of water –

And so he cursed the sea for a spell,
it licked his footprints in the sand
like a wounded dog.

And then he came down
and patted
the tiny immense mirror of the sea.

There you go, water, he said,
and went his way.

At first that conclusion might seem just coy but it is not so because its good humour is not evasiveness but a true psychological twist. It implies that man must and naturally can 'accept the universe'; that attempts by the will or the ego or even perhaps the Ministry of Truth to pervert man's indigenous genetic at-homeness in the world are sooner or later doomed to cave in to his stronger, submerged sense of belonging. And this kind of emotional reliability, this obedience to what is generally true, constitutes one of the main attractions of Holub's work. There is a charmer in this poet, certainly, but the charmer is kept in line by a sort of parental rectitude in another part of himself which is inhabited by a giver of good intellectual example. 'Zito the Magician' (in the Penguin selection) is a symptomatic poem, where Zito could stand for Holub's pattern of the artist – the man who may exercise his imaginative prerogative only up to a certain point: he may amuse his emperor by dazzling and innocuous fictions, thinking up a black star and dry water, but there comes a point when the limits of the magician's performance must be acknowledged:

Then along comes a student and asks: Think up sine alpha
greater than one.

And Zito grows pale and sad: Terribly sorry. Sine is between
plus one and minus one. Nothing you can do about that.

[*49*]

And he leaves the great royal empire, quietly weaves his way
through the throng of courtiers, to his home in a nutshell.

A parable about a man who inhabits the realms of both art and
science, certainly. But also an Aesopic tale of the artist in a
totalitarian state. Holub's well-braced stance in the world, his
suspecting weather-eye, the impression he gives of watchful
self-reliance – these things could be a result of pressures and
skills he knows as a citizen within a one-party system, in a
world of censors and official expectations. Yet this bounded
condition makes him all the more anxious to preserve his inner
freedom, and all the stricter in his vigilance over the way that
freedom is to be exercised. He is often antic but hardly
frivolous. His anti-literary note is derived partly from one
tradition of Czech poetry, partly (it has been suggested) from
the example of William Carlos Williams. But whereas with
Williams the matter of style and idiom almost made up a whole
theme and subject unto itself, with Holub I suspect the self-
consciousness is much less. The tone of the poetry seems to be
nearer to the on-the-wing colloquialism of Lawrence's *Pansies*,
although we have to imagine Lawrence's impetuous up-front-
ness allied to a mind at once allusive and elliptical. Lawrence,
for example, could have evoked the carrion-haunting, egg-
laying life of 'The Fly', but he would never have imagined the
germ life of the creature within the phantasmagoria of history,
as Holub does unforgettably in a poem that shows him at his
very best, rich and restless, equidistant from satire and surrea-
lism, ploughing a deeper emotional furrow than usual. We
forget that we are reading a translation, perhaps because the
geography of the poem and the *dramatis personae* revive the
charred memories of Shakespearian history plays. Whatever
the reason, it has found in English an emotional and literary
climate that suits it perfectly.

> She sat on the willow bark
> watching
> part of the battle of Crécy,
> the shrieks,
> the moans,

the wails,
the trampling and tumbling.

During the fourteenth charge
of the French cavalry
she mated
with a brown-eyed male fly
from Vadincourt.

She rubbed her legs together
sitting on a disembowelled horse
meditating
on the immortality of flies.

Relieved she alighted
on the blue tongue
of the Duke of Clervaux.

When silence settled
and the whisper of decay
softly circled the bodies

and just
a few arms and legs
twitched under the trees

she began to lay her eggs
on the single eye
of Johann Uhr,
the Royal Armourer.

And so it came to pass –
she was eaten by a swift
fleeing
from the fires of Estrés.

This has the wire-sculpture economy of much Eastern European poetry but seems to have fallen into place in translation with all its imaginative freight perfectly preserved.

Not that the other poems feel out of place. There is a clarity and wryness about the sequence of 'Brief Reflections' that reveal Holub at his Parnassian best – not poems of the first intensity but the bonuses of his secured idiom. And it is in

[51]

another sequence of 'Prolonged Reflections' (done in prose) that Holub insists on the central function of his stripped-down, un-sublime poetics and finds an image of his truth-telling responsibilities as scientist and artist. Both are guardians of the right names of things and both find themselves driven to reflect 'On the Necessity of Truth'. Typically, this resonant title gives way to a story about a man in a cinema, shouting protests at and against the voice of the soundtrack, the narrator in a natural history film who keeps calling a muskrat a beaver:

> Nobody can tolerate crookneck squash being called turnips, or Sirius Aldebaran. The right name is the first step toward the truth which makes things things and us us. Which conjures away any peril of the nameless things, and helps us live. And such hairsplitting in natural history is on the one hand a phenomenon of essential human features, and an element of science on the other.

These reflections translate well because the poetry is, as it were, in the plotting. They are games of knowledge, typical of Holub's poetry in that they are eager to tell truths about the nature of reality. The primary covenant of this work is not with literary convention or the history of culture – though it forages in the cultural past for its figures, as, for example, when a team of puppets perform the Gilgamesh epic, or when a transit bus takes on aspects of Charon's barge. It quarrels with classicism in the same spirit as Czeslaw Milosz quarrels with it in his resolute book on *The Witness of Poetry* where he detects the constantly threatening 'temptation to surrender to merely graceful writing' as a disabling part of the heritage of classicism. Classicism, in this definition, becomes a negative aspect of the Horatian *dulce*, a matter of conventional ornament, a protective paradigm of the way things are, drawn from previous readings of the world which remain impervious to new perceptions and which are therefore deleterious to the growth of consciousness. Both of these writers would assent to the line in Brian Friel's play, *Translations*, where a character laments the way 'a civilization can become imprisoned in a linguistic contour that no longer matches the landscape of fact'.

Holub is in pursuit of 'the fully exposed poem'. At one

moment, his writings have the kaleidoscopic glamour of chemical process, at the next the mocking realism of the quick-change artist. They brim with inventiveness and are driven by a logic generated out of the friction between two contradictory, equally commanding truths: annihilation is certain and therefore all human endeavour is futile – annihilation is certain and therefore all human endeavour is victorious.

Atlas of Civilization

At the very end of his life, Socrates' response to his recurring dream, which had instructed him to 'practise the art', was to begin to put the fables of Aesop into verse. It was, of course, entirely in character for the philosopher to be attracted to fictions whose *a priori* function was to expose the shape of things, and it was proper that even this slight brush with the art of poetry should involve an element of didacticism. But imagine what the poems of Socrates would have been like if, instead of doing adaptations, he had composed original work during those hours before he took the poison. It is unlikely that he would have broken up his lines to weep; indeed, it is likely that he would not only have obeyed Yeats's injunction on this score, but that he would have produced an *œuvre* sufficient to confound the master's claim that 'The intellect of man is forced to choose/ Perfection of the life or of the work'.

It would be an exaggeration to say that the work of the Polish poet Zbigniew Herbert* could pass as a substitute for such an ideal poetry of reality. Yet in the exactions of its logic, the temperance of its tone, and the extremity and equanimity of its recognitions, it does resemble what a twentieth-century poetic version of the examined life might be. Admittedly, in all that follows here, it is an English translation rather than the Polish

Barbarian in the Garden, translated by Michael March and Jaroslaw Anders, Carcanet, 1986.

Selected Poems, translated by Czeslaw Milosz and Peter Dale Scott, with an introduction by A. Alvarez, Ecco Press, 1986.

Report from the Besieged City and Other Poems, translated with an introduction and notes by John Carpenter and Bogdana Carpenter, Ecco Press, 1986.

[54]

original which is being praised or pondered, but what convinces one of the universal resource of Herbert's writing is just this ability which it possesses to lean, without toppling, well beyond the plumb of its native language.

Herbert himself, however, is deeply attracted to that which does not lean but which 'trusts geometry, simple numerical rule, the wisdom of the square, balance and weight'. He rejoices in the discovery that 'Greek architecture originated in the sun' and that 'Greek architects knew the art of measuring with shadows. The north–south axis was marked by the shortest shadow cast by the sun's zenith. The problem was to trace the perpendicular, the holy east–west direction.' Hence the splendid utility of Pythagoras' theorem, and the justice of Herbert's observation that 'the architects of the Doric temples were less concerned with beauty than with the chiselling of the world's order into stone'.

These quotations come from the second essay in *Barbarian in the Garden*, a collection of ten meditations on art and history which masquerade as 'travel writings' in so far as nine of them are occasioned by visits to specific places, including Lascaux, Sicily, Arles, Orvieto, Siena, Chartres, and the various resting places of the paintings of Piero della Francesca. A tenth one also begins and ends at a single pungent site, the scorched earth of an island in the Seine where on 18 March 1314, Jacques de Molay, Grand Master of the Order of the Templars, was burned at the stake along with Geoffroi de Charney and thirty-six brothers of their order. Yet this section of the book also travels to a domain with which Herbert is already too familiar: the domain of tyranny, with its police precision, mass arrests, tortures, self-inculpations, purges, and eradications, all those methods which already in the fourteenth century had begun to 'enrich the repertoire of power'.

Luckily, the poet's capacity for admiration is more than equal to his perception of the atrocious, and *Barbarian in the Garden* is an ironical title. This 'barbarian' who makes his pilgrimage to the sacred places is steeped in the culture and history of classical and medieval Europe, and even though there is situated at the centre of his consciousness a large burnt-out zone inscribed 'what we have learned in modern times and must never forget even though we need hardly dwell upon it', this very consciousness can still muster a sustaining half-trust in man as a civilizer and keeper of civilizations. The book is full of lines which sing out in the highest registers of intellectual rapture. In Paestum, 'Greek temples live under the golden sun of geometry'. In Orvieto, to enter the cathedral is a surprise, 'so much does the façade differ from the interior – as though the gate of life full of birds and colours led into a cold, austere eternity'. In the presence of a Piero della Francesca: 'He is . . . like a figurative painter who has passed through a cubist phase.' In the presence of Piero's *Death of Adam* in Arezzo: 'The entire scene appears Hellenic, as though the Old Testament were composed by Aeschylus.'

But Herbert never gets too carried away. The ground-hugging sturdiness which he recognizes and cherishes in archaic buildings has its analogue in his own down-to-earthness. His love of 'the quiet chanting of the air and the immense planes' does not extend so far as to constitute a betrayal of the human subject, in thrall to gravity and history. His imagination is slightly less skyworthy than that of his great compatriot Czeslaw Milosz, who has nevertheless recognized in the younger poet a kindred spirit and as long ago as 1968 translated, with Peter Dale Scott, the now reissued *Selected Poems*. Deliciously susceptible as he is to the '*lucidus ordo* – an eternal order of light and balance' in the work of Piero, Herbert is still greatly pleasured by the density and miscellany of what he finds in a book by Piero's contemporary, the architect and humanist Leon Battista Alberti:

> Despite its classical structure, technical subjects are mixed with anecdotes and trivia. We may read about foundations, building-sites, bricklaying, doorknobs, wheels, axes, levers, hacks, and how to 'exterminate and destroy snakes, mosquitoes, bed-bugs, fleas, mice, moths and other importunate night creatures'.

Clearly, although he quotes Berenson elsewhere, Herbert would be equally at home with a builder. He is very much the poet of a workers' republic in so far as he possesses a natural affinity with those whose eyes narrow in order to effect an operation or a calculation rather than to study a refinement. Discussing the self-portrait of Luca Signorelli which that painter entered in *The Coming of the Anti-Christ* (in the duomo at Orvieto) alongside a portrait of his master, Fra Angelico, Herbert makes a distinction between the two men. He discerns how Signorelli's eyes 'are fixed upon reality . . . Beside him, Fra Angelico dressed in a cassock gazes inwards. Two glances: one visionary, the other observant.' It is a distinction which suggests an equivalent division within the poet, deriving from the co-existence within his own deepest self of two conflicting strains. These were identified by A. Alvarez in his introduction to the original 1968 volume as the tender-minded and the tough-minded, and it is some such crossing of a natural readiness to consent upon an instinctive suspicion which constitutes the peculiar fibre of Herbert's mind and art.

There is candour and there is concentration. His vigilance never seems to let up and we feel sure that if he is enjoying himself in print (which is memory), then the original experience was also enjoyed in similar propitious conditions. All through *Barbarian in the Garden*, the tender-minded, desiring side of his nature is limpidly, felicitously engaged. In a church in a Tuscan village where 'there is hardly room enough for a coffin', he encounters a Madonna. 'She wears a simple, high-waisted dress open from breast to knees. Her left hand rests on a hip, a country bridesmaid's gesture; her right hand touches her belly but without a trace of licentiousness.' In a similar fashion, as he reports his ascent of the tower of Senlis Cathedral, the writing unreels like a skein long stored in the cupboard of the senses. 'Patches of lichen, grass between the stones, and bright yellow flowers'; then, high up on a gallery, an 'especially beautiful Eve. Coarse-grained, big-eyed and plump. A heavy plait of hair falls on her wide, warm back.'

Writing of this sort which ensures, in Neruda's words, that 'the reality of the world should not be underprized', is valuable in itself, but what reinforces Herbert's contribution and takes it far beyond being just another accomplished print-out of a cultivated man's impressions is his sceptical historical sense of the world's unreliability. He is thus as appreciative of the unfinished part of Siena Cathedral and as unastonished by it as he is entranced by what is exquisitely finished: 'The majestic plan remained unfulfilled, interrupted by the Black Death and errors in construction.' The elegance of that particular zeugma should not blind us to its outrage; the point is that Herbert is constantly wincing in the jaws of a pincer created by the mutually indifferent intersection of art and suffering. Long habituation to this crux has bred in him a tone which is neither vindictive against art nor occluded to pain. It predisposes him to quote Cicero on the colonies of Sicily as 'an ornamental band sewn on to the rough cloth of barbarian lands, a golden band that was frequently stained with blood'. And it enables him to strike his own jocund, unnerving sentences, like this one about the Baglioni family of Perugia: 'They were vengeful and cruel, though refined enough to slaughter their enemies on beautiful summer evenings.'

Once more, this comes from his essay on Piero della Francesca, and it is in writing about this beloved painter that Herbert articulates most clearly the things we would want to say about himself as an artist: 'The harmonized background and the principle of tranquillity', 'the rule of the demon of perspective', the viewing of the world as 'through a pane of ice', an 'epic impassiveness', a quality which is 'impersonal, supra-individual'. All these phrases apply, at one time or another, to Herbert's poetry and adumbrate a little more the shapes of his 'tough-mindedness'. Yet they should not be taken to suggest any culpable detachment or abstraction. The impassiveness, the perspective, the impersonality, the tranquillity, all derive from his unblindable stare at the facts of pain, the recurrence of injustice and catastrophe; but they derive also from a deep love for the whole Western tradition of religion, literature, and art, which have remained open to him as a spiritual resource, helping him to stand his ground. Herbert is as familiar as any twentieth-century writer with the hollow men and has seen more broken columns with his eyes than most literary people have seen in their imaginations, but this does not end up in a collapse of his trust in the humanist endeavour. On the contrary, it summons back to mind the whole dimensions of that endeavour and enforces it once more upon your awareness for the great boon which it is (not *was*), something we may have thought of as vestigial before we began reading these books but which, by the time we have finished, stands before our understanding once again like 'a cathedral in the wilderness'.

Barbarian in the Garden was first published in Polish in 1962 and is consequently the work of a much younger man (Herbert was born in 1924) than the one who wrote the poems of *Report from the Besieged City*. But the grave, laconic, instructive prose, translated with such fine regard for cadence and concision by Michael March and Jaroslaw Anders, is recognizably the work of the same writer. It would be wrong to say that in the meantime Herbert has matured, since from the beginning the look he turned upon experience was penetrating, judicial, and absolutely in earnest; but it could be said that he has grown even more secure in his self-possession and now begins to resemble an old judge who has developed the benevolent aspect of a daydreamer while retaining all the readiness and spring of a crouched lion. Where the poems of the reissued *Selected Poems* carry within themselves the battened-down energy and enforced caution of the situation from which they arose in Poland in the 1950s, the poems of the latest volume allow themselves a much greater latitude of voice. They are physically longer, less impacted, more social and genial in tone. They occur within a certain spaciousness, in an atmosphere of winnowed comprehension. One thinks again of the *lucidus ordo*, of that 'golden sun of geometry'; yet because of the body heat of the new poetry, its warm breath which keeps stirring the feather of our instinctive nature, one thinks also of Herbert's eloquent valediction to the prehistoric caves of the Dordogne:

I returned from Lascaux by the same road I arrived. Though I had stared into the abyss of history, I did not emerge from an alien world. Never before had I felt a stronger or more reassuring conviction: I am a citizen of the earth, an inheritor not only of the Greeks and Romans but of almost the whole of infinity . . .

The road opened to the Greek temples and the Gothic cathedrals. I walked towards them feeling the warm touch of the Lascaux painter on my palm.

[59]

It is no wonder, therefore, that Mr Cogito, the poet's alibi/alias/
persona/ventriloquist's doll/permissive correlative, should be
so stubbornly attached to the senses of sight and touch. In the
second section of 'Eschatological Forebodings of Mr Cogito',
after Herbert's several musings about his ultimate fate –
'probably he will sweep/ the great square of Purgatory' – he
imagines him taking courses in the eradication of earthly habits.
And yet, in spite of these angelic debriefing sessions, Mr Cogito

> continues to see
> a pine on a mountain slope
> dawn's seven candlesticks
> a blue-veined stone
>
> he will yield to all tortures
> gentle persuasions
> but to the end he will defend
> the magnificent sensation of pain
>
> and a few weathered images
> on the bottom of the burned-out eye
>
> 3
>
> who knows
> perhaps he will manage
> to convince the angels
> he is incapable
> of heavenly
> service
>
> and they will permit him to return
> by an overgrown path
> at the shore of a white sea
> to the cave of the beginning

The poles of the beginning and the end are crossing and at the
very moment when he strains to imagine himself at the
shimmering circumference of the imaginable, Mr Cogito finds
himself collapsing back into the palpable centre. Yet all this is
lightened of its possible portentousness because it is happening
not to 'humanity' or 'mankind' but to Mr Cogito. Mr Cogito

operates sometimes like a cartoon character, a cosmic Don Quixote or matchstick Sisyphus; sometimes like a discreet convention whereby the full frontal of the autobiographical 'I' is veiled. It is in this latter role that he is responsible for one of the book's most unforgettable poems, 'Mr Cogito – The Return', which, along with 'The Abandoned', 'Mr Cogito's Soul', and the title poem, strikes an unusually intimate and elegiac note.

Mostly, however, Mr Cogito figures as a stand-in for experimental, undaunted *Homo sapiens*, or, to be more exact, as a representative of the most courageous, well-disposed, and unremittingly intelligent members of the species. The poems where he fulfils this function are no less truly pitched and sure of their step than the ones I have just mentioned; in fact, they are more brilliant as intellectual reconnaissance and more deadly as political resistance; they are on the offensive, and to read them is to put oneself through the mill of Herbert's own personal selection process, to be tested for one's comprehension of the necessity of refusal, one's ultimate gumption and awareness. This poetry is far more than 'dissident'; it gives no consolation to papmongers or propagandists of whatever stripe. Its whole intent is to devastate those arrangements which are offered as truth by power's window-dressers everywhere. It can hear the screech of the fighter bomber behind the righteous huffing of the official spokesman, yet it is not content with just an exposé or an indictment. Herbert always wants to probe past official versions of collective experience into the final ring of the individual's perception and endurance. He does so in order to discover whether that inner citadel of human being is a selfish bolt hole or an attentive listening post. To put it another way, he would not be all that interested in discovering the black box after the crash, since he would far prefer to be able to monitor the courage and conscience of each passenger during the minutes before it. Thus, in their introduction, John and Bogdana Carpenter quote him as follows:

You understand I had words in abundance to express my rebellion and protest. I might have written something of this sort: 'O you cursed, damned people, so and sos, you kill innocent people, wait and a just punishment will fall on you'. I didn't say this because I wanted to bestow a broader dimension on the specific, individual, experienced situation, or rather, to show its deeper, general human perspectives.

This was always his impulse, and it is a pleasure to watch his strategies for showing 'deeper, general human perspectives' develop. In the *Selected Poems*, dramatic monologues and adaptations of Greek myth were among his preferred approaches. There can be no more beautiful expression of necessity simultaneously recognized and lamented than the early 'Elegy of Fortinbras', just as there can be no poem more aghast at those who have power to hurt and who then do hurt than 'Apollo and Marsyas'. Both works deserve to be quoted in full, but here is the latter, in the translation of Czeslaw Milosz:

> The real duel of Apollo
> with Marsyas
> (absolute ear
> versus immense range)
> takes place in the evening
> when as we already know
> the judges
> have awarded victory to the god
>
> bound tight to a tree
> meticulously stripped of his skin
> Marsyas
> howls
> before the howl reaches his tall ears
> he reposes in the shadow of that howl
>
> shaken by a shudder of disgust
> Apollo is cleaning his instrument
>
> only seemingly
> is the voice of Marsyas
> monotonous
> and composed of a single vowel
> Aaa

in reality
Marsyas relates
the inexhaustible wealth
of his body

bald mountains of liver
white ravines of aliment
rustling forests of lung
sweet hillocks of muscle
joints bile blood and shudders
the wintry wind of bone
over the salt of memory
shaken by a shudder of disgust
Apollo is cleaning his instrument

now to the chorus
is joined the backbone of Marsyas
in principle the same A
only deeper with the addition of rust

this is already beyond the endurance
of the god with nerves of artificial fibre

along a gravel path
hedged with box
the victor departs
wondering
whether out of Marsyas' howling
there will not some day arise
a new kind
of art – let us say – concrete

suddenly
at his feet
falls a petrified nightingale

he looks back
and sees
that the hair of the tree to which Marsyas was fastened

is white
completely

About suffering, he was never wrong, this young master. The Polish experience of cruelty lies behind the poem, and when it first appeared it would have had the extra jangle of anti-poetry about it. There is the affront of the subject matter, the flirtation with horror-movie violence, and the conscious avoidance of anything 'tender-minded'. Yet the triumph of the thing is that while it remains set upon an emotional collison course, it still manages to keep faith with 'whatever shares/ The eternal reciprocity of tears'. Indeed, this is just the poetry which Yeats would have needed to convince him of the complacency of his objection to Wilfred Owen's work (passive suffering is not a subject for poetry), although, in fact, it is probably only Wilfred Owen (tender-minded) and Yeats (tough-minded) who brought into poetry in English a 'vision of reality' as adequate to our times as this one.

'Apollo and Marsyas' is a poem, not a diagram. By now, the anti-poetry element has evaporated or been inhaled so that in spite of that devastating A-note, the poem's overall music dwells in the sorrowing registers of cello or pibroch. The petrified nightingale, the tree with white hair, the monotonous *Aaa* of the new art, each of these inventions is as terrible as it is artful, each is uttered from the dry well of an objective voice. The demon of perspective rules while the supra-individual principle reads history through a pane of Francescan ice, tranquilly, impassively, as if the story were chiselled into stone.

The most celebrated instance of Herbert's capacity to outface what the stone ordains occurs in his poem 'Pebble'. Once again, this is an *ars poetica*, but the world implied by the poem would exclude any discourse that was so fancied-up as to admit a term like *ars poetica* in the first place. Yet 'Pebble' is several steps ahead of satire and even one or two steps beyond the tragic gesture. It is written by a poet who grew up, as it were, under the white-haired tree but who possessed no sense either of the oddity or the election of his birthright. In so far as it accepts the universe with a sort of disappointed relief – as though at the last minute faith were to renege on its boast that it could move mountains and settle back into stoicism – it demonstrates the truth of Patrick Kavanagh's contention that tragedy is half-born comedy. The poem's force certainly resides in its impersonality, yet its tone is almost ready to play itself on through into the altogether more lenient weather of personality itself.

> The pebble
> is a perfect creature
>
> equal to itself
> mindful of its limits
>
> filled exactly
> with pebbly meaning
>
> with a scent which does not remind one of anything
> does not frighten anything away does not arouse desire
>
> its ardour and coldness
> are just and full of dignity
>
> I feel a heavy remorse
> when I hold it in my hand
> and its noble body
> is permeated by false warmth
>
>   – Pebbles cannot be tamed
>   to the end they will look at us
>   with a calm and very clear eye

This has about it all the triumph and completion of the 'finished man among his enemies'. You wonder where else an art that is so contained and self-verifying can possibly go – until you open *Report from the Besieged City*. There you discover that the perfect moral health of the earlier poetry was like the hard pure green of the ripening apple: now the core of the thing is less packed with tartness and the whole *œuvre* seems to mellow and sway on the bough of some tree of unforbidden knowledge.

There remain, however, traces of the acerbic observer; this, for example, in the poem where Damastes (also known as Procrustes) speaks:

> I invented a bed with the measurements of a perfect man
> I compared the travellers I caught with this bed

it was hard to avoid – I admit – stretching limbs cutting legs
the patients died but the more there were who perished
the more I was certain my research was right
the goal was noble progress demands victims

This voice is stereophonic in that we are listening to it through
two speakers, one from the set-up Damastes, the other from
the privileged poet, and we always know whose side we are
on. We are meant to read the thing exactly as it is laid out
for us. We stand with Signorelli at the side of the picture,
observantly. We are still, in other words, in the late spring of
impersonality. But when we come to the poem on the Emperor
Claudius, we are in the summer of fullest personality. It is not
that Herbert has grown lax or that any phoney tolerance –
understanding all and therefore forgiving all – has infected his
attitude. It is more that he has eased his own grimness, as if
realizing that the stern brows he turns upon the world merely
contribute to the weight of the world's anxiety instead of
lightening it; therefore, he can afford to become more genial
personally without becoming one whit less impersonal in his
judgements and perceptions. So, in his treatment of 'The
Divine Claudius', the blood and the executions and the infernal
whimsicality are not passed over, yet Herbert ends up speaking for his villain with a less than usually forked tongue:

I expanded the frontiers of the empire
by Brittany Mauretania
and if I recall correctly Thrace

my death was caused by my wife Agrippina
and an uncontrollable passion for boletus
mushrooms – the essence of the forest – became the essence of
    death

descendants – remember with proper respect and honour
at least one merit of the divine Claudius
I added new signs and sounds to our alphabet
expanded the limits of speech that is the limits of freedom

the letters I discovered – beloved daughters – Digamma and
    Antisigma

led my shadow
as I pursued the path with tottering steps to the dark land of
  Orkus

There is more of the inward gaze of Fra Angelico here, and
indeed, all through the new book, Herbert's mind is fixed
constantly on last things. Classical and Christian visions of the
afterlife are drawn upon time and again, and in 'Mr Cogito –
Notes from the House of the Dead', we have an opportunity of
hearing how the terrible cry of Marsyas sounds in the new
acoustic of the later work. Mr Cogito, who lies with his fellows
'in the depths of the temple of the absurd', hears there, at ten
o'clock in the evening, 'a voice// masculine/ slow/ commanding/
the rising/ of the dead'. The second section of the poem
proceeds:

> we called him Adam
> meaning taken from the earth
>
> at ten in the evening
> when the lights were switched off
> Adam would begin his concert
>
> to the ears of the profane
> it sounded
> like the howl of a person in fetters
>
> for us
> an epiphany
>
> he was
> anointed
> the sacrificial animal
> author of psalms
>
> he sang
> the inconceivable desert
> the call of the abyss
> the noose on the heights
>
> Adam's cry
> was made

[67]

of two or three vowels
stretched out like ribs on the horizon

This new Adam has brought us as far as the old Marsyas took us, but now the older Herbert takes up the burden and, in a third section, brings the poem further still:

after a few concerts
he fell silent

the illumination of his voice
lasted a brief time

he didn't redeem
his followers

they took Adam away
or he retreated
into eternity

the source
of the rebellion
was extinguished

and perhaps
only I
still hear
the echo
of his voice

more and more slender
quieter
further and further away

like music of the spheres
the harmony of the universe

so perfect
it is inaudible.

Mr Cogito's being depends upon such cogitations (one remembers his defence of 'the magnificent sensation of pain'), though unlike Hamlet, in Fortinbras's elegy, who 'crunched the air only to vomit', Mr Cogito's digestion of the empty spaces is

curiously salutary. Reading these poems is a beneficent experience: they amplify immensely Thomas Hardy's assertion that
'If a way to the Better there be, it exacts a full look at the Worst'.
But the end of the book, after such undaunted poems at 'The
Power of Taste' – 'Yes taste/ in which there are fibres of soul the
cartilage of conscience' – and such tender ones as 'Lament', to
the memory of his mother – 'she sails on the bottom of a boat
through foamy nebulas' – after these and the other poems I
have mentioned, and many more which I have not, the reader
feels the kind of gratitude the gods of Troy must have felt when
they saw Aeneas creep from the lurid fires, bearing ancestry on
his shoulders and the sacred objects in his hands.

The book's true subject is survival of the valid self, of the city,
of the good and the beautiful; or rather, the subject is the
responsibility of each person to ensure that survival. So it is
possible in the end to think that a poet who writes so ethically
about the *res publica* might even be admitted by Plato as first
laureate of the ideal republic; though it is also necessary to think
that through to the point where this particular poet would be
sure to decline the office as a dangerous compromise:

> now as I write these words the advocates of conciliation
> have won the upper hand over the party of inflexibles
> a normal hesitation of moods fate still hangs in the balance
>
> cemeteries grow larger the number of the defenders is
>   smaller
> yet the defence continues it will continue to the end
> and if the City falls but a single man escapes
> he will carry the City within himself on the roads of exile
> he will be the City
>
> we look in the face of hunger the face of fire face of death
> worst of all – the face of betrayal
>
> and only our dreams have not been humiliated
>
> (1982)

The title poem, to which these lines form the conclusion, is
pivoted at the moment of martial law and will always belong in
the annals of patriotic Polish verse. It witnesses new develop-

ments and makes old connections within the native story and is only one of several poems throughout the volume which sweep the strings of Polish national memory. If I have been less attentive to this domestic witnessing function of the book than I might have been, it is not because I undervalue that function of Herbert's poetry. On the contrary, it is precisely because I am convinced of its obdurate worth on the home front that I feel free to elaborate in the luxurious margin. Anyhow, John and Bogdana Carpenter have annotated the relevant dates and names so that the reader is kept alert to the allusions and connections which provide the book's oblique discharge of political energy. As well as providing this editorial service, they seem to have managed the task of translating well; I had no sense of their coming between me and the poem's first life, no sense of their having interfered.

Zbigniew Herbert is a poet with all the strengths of an Antaeus, yet he finally emerges more like the figure of an Atlas. Refreshed time and again by being thrown back upon his native earth, standing his ground determinedly in the local plight, he nevertheless shoulders the whole sky and scope of human dignity and responsibility. These various translations provide a clear view of the power and beauty of the profile which he has established, and leave no doubt about the essential function which his work performs, that of keeping a trustworthy poetic canopy, if not a perfect heaven, above our vulnerable heads.

Osip and Nadezhda Mandelstam

'After slapping Alexei Tolstoi in the face, M. immediately returned to Moscow. From there he rang Akhmatova every day, begging her to come.' It would be hard to find a more dramatic opening than these first sentences of Nadezhda Mandelstam's *Hope against Hope*. The panic of the occasion is matched only by her pride in recollection, even though what is being recollected is the fatal story of her husband, the poet Osip Mandelstam – the M. of Nadezhda's indomitable memoir.

In 1932, Alexei Tolstoi had presided over a 'comrades' court' set up by the Writers' Union to hear Mandelstam's complaint against the novelist Sargidzhan. The Mandelstams were by then in disrepute with the Soviet authorities and the novelist and his wife had been set to spy on them in their apartment building. As a result of the ensuing proximity, suspicion and hostility, Sargidzhan had finally hit Nadezhda 'very hard'. The

Stone by Osip Mandelstam, translated by Robert Tracy. Princeton University Press (1981)

Journey to Armenia by Osip Mandelstam, translated by Clarence Brown, with an introduction by Bruce Chatwin. Next Editions and Faber (1981)

Selected Poems by Osip Mandelstam, translated by Clarence Brown and W. S. Merwin. Oxford University Press (1973) and Penguin (1977)

The Prose of Osip Mandelstam translated by Clarence Brown. Princeton University Press (1967)

The Complete Critical Prose and Letters translated by Jane Gary Harris and Constance Link. Ardis (1979)

Hope against Hope by Nadezhda Mandelstam, translated by Max Hayward. Harvill Press (1971) and Penguin (1976)

Hope Abandoned by Nadezhda Mandelstam, translated by Max Hayward. Harvill Press (1974) and Penguin (1976)

Mandelstam by Clarence Brown. Cambridge University Press (1973)

court found the 'the whole affair was a survival from the bourgeois system and that both sides were equally to blame'. A commotion then started in the court, the judges took refuge in a room, but in the end Tolstoi burst out through the crowd calling: 'Leave me alone, leave me alone. I couldn't do anything! We had our orders.' Two years later Osip delivered the retaliatory smack. In Nadezhda's words, Mandelstam thought that 'the man ought not to have obeyed the orders. Not such orders. That's the whole story.'

It is, of course, far from being the whole story. The slap was the outward sign of an inner grace which had returned to Mandelstam in the middle of 1930 when he made his journey to Armenia. In the course of his travels there, the sense of being right, the inner freedom without which he could not summon his poetry, was restored and his five years' poetic silence was broken. Along with the poetry came the power not to obey orders, and almost, it would seem, as a proof to himself that the power was absolute, Mandelstam later wrote his uncharacteristically explicit and 'political' poem against Stalin, 'the Kremlin mountaineer'. It was, in fact, this poem that was the real cause of Mandelstam's first arrest a day or two after the face-slapping incident: David had faced Goliath with eight stony couplets in his sling.

The Moscow apartment was searched by the secret police, Mandelstam was taken to their headquarters in the Lubianka Prison, interrogated, and sentenced to three years of exile in Cherdyn, where, in a deranged state, he attempted suicide by throwing himself from a hospital window. Then the 'miracle', as Nadezhda Mandelstam calls it, happened. As a result of Stalin's personal interest in the case, an interest kept warm by Pasternak's subtle handling of a phone call from the dictator himself, the sentence was commuted to exile in some town in European Russia, excluding the principal cities.

'Suddenly M. remembered that Leonov, a biologist at Tashkent University, had said good things about Voronezh . . . Leonov's father worked there as a prison doctor. "Who knows, perhaps we shall need a prison doctor," said M., and we decided on Voronezh.' The light-hearted tone seems to have been characteristic. And to a man who deliberately travelled light, who consciously identified himself with the *raznochintsi*, those 'upstart intellectuals' of the 1860s, and who at this stage was imbued with Dante to the extent that he found his own practice of composing poetry by mouth and often on foot prefigured in the master – 'the step, linked to the breathing and saturated with thought: this Dante understands as the beginning of prosody' – to such a man, who could also wonder 'quite seriously, how many ox-hide shoes, how many sandals Alighieri wore out in the course of his poetic work, wandering about on the goat-paths of Italy', the prospect of exile was not altogether disabling. However, this illusory sense of well-being arose only when he had regained his mental balance: during his hallucinations on the journey from Moscow to Cherdyn, and during his confinement in the hospital there, Mandelstam lived in terror, in an unmitigated awareness that he was doomed. Once his wife and the housekeeper had to hide the clock from him, to allay his demented conviction that executioners would arrive in the ward to shoot him at exactly six o'clock.

Nadezhda's awareness was equally unmitigated, but was sustained in the daylight of a sane consciousness. Suddenly she became a guerrilla of the imagination, devoted to the cause of poetry, to the preservation of her husband's achievement and, in particular, to the preservation of his manuscripts. The words that formed part of the commuted sentence which was meant to 'isolate' and 'preserve' the poet might equally apply to the task she instinctively and religiously – the word is not too strong – undertook the moment the secret police entered their apartment. From then on, she was like a hunted priest in penal times, travelling dangerously with the altar-stone of the forbidden faith, disposing the manuscripts for safe keeping among the secret adherents. And inevitably, having consecrated herself a guardian, she was destined to become a witness.

As a consequence, the mature work of a great poet survived, and two of the most fortifying books of our times, Nadezhda Mandelstam's *Hope against Hope* and *Hope Abandoned* (the titles constitute puns on her first name, which means 'hope' in Russian), were finally written in the late 1960s. In these books, we have a devastating indictment of most of what happened in post-revolutionary Russia and, more intimately, the story of

Mandelstam's Voronezh exile, his return to Moscow in 1937, his re-arrest and deportation to a labour camp: 'My first book was *Stone* and my last will be stone, too.' He died just before his forty-eighth birthday in a transit camp near Vladivostok, having travelled the five and a half thousand miles from Moscow in a prisoner transport train. The official cause of his death was given as 'heart failure': Mandelstam did suffer from a heart complaint, though he may in fact have died of typhus. His widow reports the way in which she was given the news:

> I was sent a notice asking me to go to the post office at Nikita Gate. Here I was handed back the parcel I had sent to M. in the camp. 'The addressee is dead,' the young lady behind the counter informed me. It would be easy enough to establish the date on which the parcel was returned to me – it was the same day on which the newspapers published the long list of Government awards – the first ever – to Soviet writers.

By then, the Mandelstam *œuvre* was complete, though it was not until the New York edition of his *Collected Works* in 1955 that anything like a complete record got into print. Before that, more than two hundred of the poems were kept alive in 'pre-Gutenberg' conditions. As far as the Soviet reader was concerned, Mandelstam was finished as a poet after the appearance in 1928 of the three books which marked the culmination of his public writing career: his *Poems*, a collection of criticism entitled *On Poetry*, and a volume containing 'The Noise of Time', his autobiographical account of childhood in St Petersburg, and the fictional title piece 'The Egyptian Stamp'. But in Voronezh the Mandelstams compiled three notebooks of the work that came after this. Nadezhda writes:

> I have often been asked about the origin of these 'Notebooks'. This was the name we used to refer to all the poems composed between 1930 and 1937 which we copied down in Voronezh in ordinary school exercise books (we were never able to get decent paper, and even these exercise books were hard to come by). The first group constituted what is now called the 'First Voronezh Note-

book' [new work done in exile, it would seem], and then all the verse composed between 1930 and 1934, which had been confiscated during the search of our apartment, was copied down into a second notebook . . . In the fall of 1936, when some more poems had accumulated, M. asked me to get a new exercise book.

In spite of his disregard for 'writing' (the word was used contemptuously to describe, among other things, informers' reports, and anyhow Mandelstam worked, not with a pen, but with his 'moving lips'), the poet had come to realize that a manuscript was more durable than a man, and that memory could provide no permanent sanctuary for poetry. From that sanctuary, nevertheless, it emerged with poignant force. After Osip's second arrest, for example, when Nadezhda worked the night shift in a textile factory in the town of Strunino, she kept herself awake by muttering the verses to herself: 'I had to commit everything to memory in case all my papers were taken away from me, or the various people I had given copies to took fright and burned them in a moment of panic.' And then there is this scene in a loft occupied by thieves, which was reported to Nadezhda by a man who had passed through the final transit camp at the same time as her husband:

> Sitting with the criminals was a man with a grey stubble of beard, wearing a yellow leather coat. He was reciting verse which L. recognized. It was Mandelstam. The criminals offered him bread and the canned stuff, and he calmly helped himself and ate. Evidently he was only afraid to eat food given him by his jailers. He was listened to in complete silence and sometimes asked to repeat a poem.

Though the older Mandelstam was to identify himself increasingly with outcasts and exiles, his first circle of friends was very much at the centre of the literary world in pre-revolutionary Petersburg. In the third chapter of *Hope Abandoned* Nadezhda implicitly affirms the importance of this early security and friendship with poets such as Nicolai Gumilev and Anna Akhmatova. The chapter is about the moral and artistic nurture

[75]

that can flow in a community of spirits who are 'truly entitled to refer to themselves as "we" '.

> I am quite convinced that without such a 'we', there can be no proper fulfilment of even the most ordinary 'I', that is, of the personality. To find its fulfilment, the 'I' needs at least two complementary dimensions: 'we' and – if it is fortunate – 'you'. I think M. was lucky to have had a moment in his life when he was linked by the pronoun 'we' with a group of others.

Against this true church of values, the heretical cliques of the Soviet establishment could not finally prevail, though they did indeed win in the short run, by shooting Gumilev (Akhmatova's first husband) in 1921, by hounding Mandelstam to exile and death, and by keeping Akhmatova silenced for decades. Nevertheless, from her vantage point in the 1960s, Nadezhda could triumphantly declare the conviction that carried her through the blackest times and could pronounce her anathema on the enemies with the unthinking authority of somebody brushing a fly from her food: 'Such cliques are not proof of the existence of a sense of fellowship, since they consist of individualists who are out to achieve only their own aims. They refer to themselves as "we", but in this context the pronoun indicates only a plurality devoid of any deeper sense or significance.' The underlying theme of the memoirs is this war between humanist values and the utilitarian system which was imposed by decree and then by terror, and the story they tell is so unrelentingly distressing that it is easy to forget the pure literary exuberance of the earliest period of Mandelstam's association with these Acmeist poets, when his main war was with the Symbolists and when his shoes had been worn out only by student travels to Paris and Heidelberg and, almost certainly, Italy.

Robert Tracy gives an account of the main influences in the air at the time of Mandelstam's first book, *Stone*, which he has translated *in toto* into rhymed verse, with a parallel Russian text, an excellent introduction and very illuminating notes. Tracy evokes the world of Mandelstam's childhood and schooling, so hyperbolically conjured by the poet himself in 'The

Noise of Time', and notes that the later sense of 'not belonging' was already present in the child's awareness of a tension between the 'Judaic chaos' of his home and the imperial world of Petersburg, 'the granite paradise of my sedate strolls'. Tracy also glances at the importance of the education in classical and Russian literature which Mandelstam received at the Tenishev School, where his most influential teacher was the Symbolist poet, V. V. Grippius, brought to unforgettable life in 'The Noise of Time':

> V.V. had established personal relations with Russian writers, splenetic and loving liaisons filled with noble enviousness, jealousy, with jocular disrespect, grievous unfairness – as is customary between the members of one family . . . The judgements of V.V. continue to hold me in their power down to the present day. The grand tour I made with him . . . has remained the only one. After that, I merely 'read a bit'.

Yet it was not with the Symbolist Grippius that he finally discovered his true poetic direction, but with the group known as the Acmeists, the most important of whom constituted that first community referred to by Nadezhda simply as 'The Three'.

The Acmeists were formed by reaction to and fission from the Symbolists. In the words of Clarence Brown, 'they called for the abandonment of the Symbolists' metaphysical dualism and for a return to the things of this world, for a classical and Mediterranean clarity as opposed to the gothic and northern haze of the Symbolists, and for a firm and virile approach to life.' Great manifesto stuff. Moreover, there was 'a determination to introduce some Mozartian – and Pushkinian – lightness into poetry', a sense of the poem as an animated structure, an equilibrium of forces, an architecture. All of which coursed and boiled in Mandelstam as a furious devotion to the physical word, the etymological memory bank, the word as its own form and content – 'the word is a bundle and meaning sticks out of it in various directions'. This brusque domestic approach, this impatience with the way Symbolism 'demoralized perception', runs through all his prose and verse. When he was at full tilt – and he never wrote without being there – his profound contact with the common, miraculous resources of the language as a phonetic instrument kept him close to the grain of the ordinary even as his tongue planed curlicues of fantastic association off that grain. His essay 'On the Nature of the Word', published in 1922 and therefore a kind of recapitulation of his first ideas, has a brilliant certainty and roguery about it, as when he delivers his famous attack on the Symbolist rose:

> The rose is a likeness of the sun, the sun is a likeness of the rose, a dove – of a girl, and a girl – of a dove. Images are gutted like scarecrows and packed with foreign content. In place of the Symbolist forest, we are left with a workshop producing scarecrows . . . Nothing is left but a terrifying quadrille of 'correspondences' nodding to one another. Eternal winking. Never a clear word, nothing but hints and reticent whispers. The rose nods to the girl, the girl to the rose. No one wants to be himself.

Against the shimmer and wobble and sylvan elusiveness of all this, Mandelstam's instinct led him to seek the reliable quarry face and the vaulted solidity of buildings. Stone became his image, hardness and design his consolation. Even as late as his *Journey to Armenia* we find him swooping with pure happiness on finds like this:

> When I was a child a stupid sort of touchiness, a false pride, kept me from ever going out to look for berries or stooping down over mushrooms. Gothic pine cones and hypocritical acorns in their monastic caps pleased me more than mushrooms. I would stroke the pine cones. They would bristle. They were trying to convince me of something. In their shelled tenderness, in their geometrical gaping I sensed the rudiments of architecture, the demon of which has accompanied me throughout my life.

Robert Tracy also discusses the significance of architecture and stone, and provides a lucid commentary on the central importance of Mandelstam's poems about buildings; and he has taken the poet's discipline to heart in his translations, attempting to keep the symmetries and pointings of rhyme and stanza. His ear is not as gifted as Mandelstam's – whose is? – and the high voltage of inner associative word-play which one understands to be so distinctive in Russian disappears. But there is much to be gained from holding on to metre and rhyme: the metaphorical basis in building is thereby preserved – though to speak too much in these building terms is probably to misrepresent the excitements of the 'moving lips'. A Russian poet once told me that the Mandelstam stanza has the resonant impact of late Yeats, so Tracy had *his* work cut out. But he rises to the occasion in, for example, the version of Poem 78:

> Sleeplessness. Homer. The sails tight.
> I have the catalogue of ships half read:
> That file of cranes, long fledgling line that spread
> And lifted once over Hellas, into flight.
>
> Like a wedge of cranes into an alien place –
> The god's spume foaming in the prince's hair.
> Where do you sail? If Helen were not there
> What would Troy matter, men of Achaean race?
>
> The sea, and Homer – it's love that moves all things.
> To whom should I listen? Homer falls silent now
> And the black sea surges toward my pillow
> Like a loud declaimer, heavily thundering.

As a rendering of a text this is more than impressive. But what makes Tracy's book invaluable is his feeling for context. His introduction has an important section, entitled 'Poetry and Quotation', where he rightly insists on the way Mandelstam's poems are 'as firmly rooted in both an historical and cultural context and in physical reality as Joyce's *Ulysses* or Eliot's *Waste Land*'. His notes to the poems will be essential for those who seek to locate this context, especially when it turns out to be other Russian poetry or Mandelstam's criticism.

Another thing that comes across in these translations is the verve and immediacy of the poems' occasions, recalling the Acmeist programme of 'this-worldness': there are poems about tennis and ice-cream and silent movies, poems that seem to jump into being on impulse. At times Tracy hits the note of casual intent with convincing ease:

When I hear the English tongue
Like a whistle, but even shriller –
I see Oliver Twist among
A heaping of office ledgers.

Go ask Charles Dickens this,
How it was in London then:
The old City with Dombey's office,
The yellow waters of the Thames.

There is a salubrious *élan* about much of the book, and the fact
that this is indeed a book, not just a selection of the significant
poems, amplifies our sense of what *Stone* really meant to its
contemporary readers. Most people interested in Mandelstam
will have known the importance of the key pieces on architecture – 'Hagia Sophia', 'Notre Dame', 'The Admiralty' – and
admired their confident and ambitious note: but to know them
side by side with other poems that are less earnestly assured is
to come to a fuller appreciation of their corroborating force. The
following poem (Number 62), which charmed me when it
appeared in W. S. Merwin and Clarence Brown's freer handling, deepened its claims by reappearing in this more literal and
metrical version:

Orioles in the woods, and the only measure
In tonic verse is to know short vowels from long.
There's a brimming over once in each year, when nature
Slowly draws itself out, like the metre in Homer's song.

This is a day that yawns like a caesura:
Quiet since dawn, and wearily drawn out;
Oxen at pasture, golden indolence to draw
From a pipe of reeds the richness of one full note.

Mandelstam's slap in the face to Alexei Tolstoi was by no means
his first contact with that member of the great family. Count
Tolstoi had emigrated after the Revolution, though he did
eventually return to Russia as 'The Red Count' and made
himself into a useful arm of the young regime. In 1923,

however, as editor of a literary supplement to the Berlin newspaper *On the Eve*, he had published Mandelstam's essay 'Humanism and the Present', and it would seem that at that point it was the poet who was on the side of the regime – or at least half ready to fool himself that he was. In retrospect, the whole piece takes on a tragic and ironical colouring.

Mandelstam begins by outlining his conception of the ideal society, which naturally turns out to have the same structure as the ideal building or poem. The stone, the word, the individual must maintain and fulfil their whole creative selves, but they must also be a part of a 'we', a 'social architecture', in order to bring their potential to its most fruitful development. Mandelstam is taking his note to some extent from the temper of the times and entering into the hunt for 'new forms': an optimistic view of the Revolution is implicit when he speaks of a new 'social Gothic: the free play of weights and forces, a human society conceived as a complex and dense architectural forest wherein everything is efficient and individual, and where every detail answers to the conception of the whole'. And yet this enhancing vision of harmony has been preceded at the start of the essay by a cruel and powerfully realized vision of the inhuman society, of those epochs when the individual life was treated as insignificant, when the social architecture was a crushing pyramid: 'Assyrian prisoners swarm like baby chicks under the feet of an enormous king; warriors personifying the power of the state inimical to man kill bound pygmies with long spears while Egyptians and Egyptian builders treat the human mass as building material in abundant supply, easily obtainable in any quantity.'

Fifteen years before his experience of transport trains and the compound of a camp, Mandelstam's prophetic soul trembles with foreknowledge, and though he valiantly holds himself in check – or is prepared for the moment to disguise the trembling from himself – the signs are everywhere. His allusion to the English concept of 'home' as a revolutionary concept is followed by the thought that that was 'a kind of revolution more deeply rooted and akin to our age than the French'. Wishful thinking. But not half as wishful as the concluding paragraphs:

[*81*]

The fact that the values of humanism have now become rare, as if taken out of circulation and hidden underground, is not a bad sign in itself. Humanistic values have merely withdrawn, concealed themselves like gold currency . . .

The transition to gold currency is the business of the future, and in the province of culture what lies before us is the replacement of temporary ideas – of paper banknotes – with the gold coinage of the European humanistic tradition; the magnificent florins of humanism will ring once again, not against the archaeologist's spade, but . . . like the jingling coins of common currency passing from hand to hand.

It may only be a chance of translation that the coin of Mandelstam's hope is the Florentine one, the currency of Dante's city, the Dante whom he would come upon in the 1930s and who would help him to live by the pure standard while false currency swirled all around him like blinding chaff.

Three years after this essay Mandelstam had stopped fooling himself about the nature of the world he was living in – but he had also stopped writing poetry. Nadezhda goes into the reasons for his five-year block, which ended in 1930, and implies that her husband's physical ailments as well as his imaginative ones may have had their origin in what was for him the central problem, the question of his relation to his times. She notes that it was when Mandelstam was being delivered the official line on poetry by the head of children's literature at the State Publishing House, and feeling he could stand the tempting voice no longer, that he heard a ringing in his ears which drowned it out – a sound which marked the onset of his first bout of angina pectoris.

During this time he supported himself by translations and by working more or less under the umbrella of various party organizations and publications, yet he was becoming more and more alienated. He felt himself to be 'a double-dealer with a divided soul', conniving with the 'new' by dealing with the officials of a literature he despised, but still committed in his deepest being to the 'old' values. Among the new men,

'Christian morality – including the ancient commandment, "Thou shalt not kill" – was blithely identified with "bourgeois" morality'. His disaffection was matched by their distrust and hostility, and it was inevitable for somebody with Mandelstam's impulsively courageous nature – and somebody living in the bracing moral air of Nadezhda's company – that a confrontation would occur.

In the spring of 1928, he made the first move in his offensive by intervening on behalf of five elderly bank clerks who were going to be executed. He harried people in government offices, but his decisive move was to send to the sympathetic Bukharin a copy of the recently published *Poems* with an inscription saying that 'every line in this book argues against what you plan to do'. Counter-attack took place that summer, when a publisher neglected to put the name of the original translators on the title page of a work which Mandelstam had revised, so that he was denounced, unjustly, as a plagiarist. After gruelling court hearings and interrogations, a commission of the Federation of Soviet Writers' Organizations found him morally to blame for the fact that the publisher had failed to make a contract with the earlier translators. The couple lost their apartment, and for the moment Mandelstam lay low.

In one of her most memorable phrases, Nadezhda describes her husband's work on a poem as a dig for 'the nugget of harmony', and in the same chapter comments that 'the search for lost words is an attempt to remember what is still to be brought into being'. During these troubled years it was as if Mandelstam had mislaid the nugget of harmony, and could not speak the lost words. But he recovered, suddenly and exultantly, in the summer and autumn of 1930, during his trip to Armenia. There he denounced the official formula for literature, 'National in form, Socialist in content', as stupid and illiterate – the formula was Stalin's – and turned away from the company of writers to spend his time with scientists and biologists. He wrote the angry, elliptical and cathartic 'Fourth Prose', which rolls the universe of his true values into a ball that is deadly as an iron *boule*, and symbolically tore off the fur coat he associated with privileges that came to those writers who fell into line with the regime: 'The race of professional writers emits a repugnant odour . . . yet it is forever close to the authorities, who find its members shelter in the red-light districts, as prostitutes. For literature is forever fulfilling a single assignment: it helps the rulers keep their soldiers in line and it helps the judges arbitrarily dispose of the condemned.' And: 'I tear off my own literary fur coat and trample it underfoot. I shall run three times around the boulevard rings of Moscow in nothing but my jacket in a 30-degree frost. I shall run away from the yellow hospital of the Komsomol arcade straight toward mortal pneumonia . . . if only not to hear the ringing of pieces of silver and the counting of printer's sheets.' He reclaimed his inner freedom, fell greedily upon the nugget, insisted on the purity and objectivity of his kind of poetry: 'making Brussels lace involves real work, but its major components, those supporting the design, are air, perforations and truancy.' He remembered what still had to be brought into being, but, as the image of 'mortal pneumonia' reveals, he did all this in the full knowledge that he would pay with his life for this healing of his divided soul.

Journey to Armenia is now available in Clarence Brown's translation, with an introduction by Bruce Chatwin. It appeared first in the Soviet magazine *Zvezda* in 1933, and was the last piece of his work that Mandelstam would see published in his lifetime. To call it travel writing is to miss the mark almost as badly as the *Pravda* reviewer who savaged Mandelstam for failing to notice 'the thriving, bustling Armenia which is joyfully building socialism'. When Mandelstam complained that he thought it impermissible for the country's leading newspaper to print 'yellow-press articles', an official rebuked him: 'Mandelstam, you are talking of *Pravda*.' 'It's not my fault if the article was published in *Pravda*,' Mandelstam replied. Obviously the cure was complete.

The reviewer hit the mark, nevertheless, even if it was for perverse reasons, when he found the discredited Acmeist mode alive in the piece: 'this is a style of speaking, writing and travelling cultivated before the Revolution' – and therefore to be extirpated. All of Mandelstam's old trust in the resources of language, his identification with the clarity and classical aura of the Mediterranean, his rejoicing in the 'Hellenic' nature of the

Russian inheritance, the ebullient philological certitude of his essay 'On the Nature of the Word' – all this was revived by his physical encounter with the Armenian language and landscape. Addenda and notes which did not find their way into the text make it clear that Mandelstam was aware of exactly what was going on in himself:

(If I accept total immersion in sound, steadfastness and vigour as time-honoured and just, my visit to Armenia has not been in vain.)

If I accept as time-honoured both the shadow of the oak tree and the shadow of the grave, and, indeed, the steadfastness of speech articulation, how shall I ever appreciate the present age?

Poetry came back to him. Indeed, the prose itself is bursting with eagerness to break out as a sequence of poems. As each sensation hits the tightly stretched drumhead of each sense, it emits waves from the omnipresent 'nugget of harmony'. Supply has been located, the gusher has been broached and capped, the linguistic hydraulics grip and shift into action all over again. As usual, the best glosses on the book are from the book itself: 'the helix of the ear becomes finer and is whorled in a different pattern'. And not just the ear, but the eye and the nose: there is a snout-twitching immediacy, a bushman's eagerness of body and instinct. What Mandelstam said of Darwin's style applies here perfectly to his own: the power of perception functions as an instrument of thought.

The nearest thing in English is Lawrence's travel writing: reading Lawrence, though, we are always aware that we are being given a lesson in how to respond. And the same is true to a lesser extent of Hopkins's notebooks, which also come to mind in this context. Lawrence does not renounce himself as purely as Mandelstam does: there is an underlying evangelical design in his most delightful annotations, whereas, with Mandelstam, the moral ground has been cleared beforehand (in the 'Fourth Prose') and he can now joyfully set about quarantining the whole world in the voluble compound of language itself. The old Christian ethos of Armenia and his own inner weather of feeling came together in a marvellous reaction that demonstrates upon the pulses the truth of his belief that 'the whole of our two-thousand-year-old culture is a setting of the world free for play'.

Journey to Armenia, then, is more than a rococo set of impressions. It is the celebration of a poet's return to his senses. It is a paean to the reality of poetry as a power as truly present in the nature of things as the power of growth itself. It is Shakespearian in the way it confounds art and nature – an identification glimpsed earlier in Poem 62 – and Bruce Chatwin rightly directs attention to the paragraph which gave such offence to the fur-coat brigade, a passage which throbs at one point with a memory of Mandelstam's first literary mentor, the Symbolist Grippius, who 'loved poems in which there were such energetic and happy rhymes as *plamen* (flame) – *kamen* (stone)': 'A plant is a sound evoked by the wand of a termenvox and it coos in a sphere oversaturated with wave processes. It is the envoy of a living thunderstorm that rages permanently in the universe – akin in equal measure to stone and lightning! A plant in the world is an event, a happening, an arrow, and not a boring, bearded development.'

Prose may be easier to translate – even this prose – than poetry. At any rate, I cannot believe we lose much by reading the book in Clarence Brown's lucid and athletic English, which gives us 'the golden currency of cognac in the secret cupboard of the mountain sun'. But underneath all the Hopkinsian carol and creation there lurked the blue-bleak embers of the fate Mandelstam knew he was embracing: 'The Armenians' fullness with life, their rude tenderness, their noble inclination for hard work, their inexplicable aversion to anything metaphysical and their splendid intimacy with the world of real things – all of this said to me: you're awake, don't be afraid of your own time, don't be sly.'

One of the lovely constants of Nadezhda Mandelstam's books is the deeply tuned love she had for Osip. They were obviously a powerful couple to encounter, and they obviously did operate very much *as* a couple. Without her, Mandelstam might have been less certainly himself, and her pride in him and her love – the love of a wife, after all, bearing its own secret wounds and fully aware of the partner's weak spots – made it possible for her to lay the whole truth open. She discusses Mandelstam's wavering fidelity to 'the three' in the early 1920s when he was prepared to write critically of Akhmatova; she tells with great insight the story of his failed attempts to write an ode to Stalin in the hope of reinstating himself to favour after the Voronezh interlude; and of his visit to the White Sea Canal in 1937 under the auspices of the Union of Soviet Writers, when a sympathetic spirit in that organization thought that Mandelstam might still save himself by delivering the socialist realism goods. Mandelstam was only able to turn out something on the landscape – a failure that Nadezhda reports with dry delight. She even reports the details of another failure, Mandelstam's affair in 1925 with Olga Vaskei: 'I am still surprised even now at the ruthless way he chose between us.'

She once kept two dogs which she described as 'savage, vicious and faithful', and the first and last adjectives of that triad apply to her record of the Soviet era, and in particular to her anatomy of the spirit of compromise and adaptability that prevailed among the tribe of comrades who wrote with ease. She was not herself a poet, though she knew everything about it and her memoirs are a poetic education in themselves, but like her husband she, too, addressed the 'reader in posterity', not as an artist but as a witness. There is a note of almost maternal joy when she relates Mandelstam's transformation, after the 'Fourth Prose' had cleared the bad air generated by the plagiarism denunciation and its aftermath:

> The two years spent on this business were rewarded a hundred times over: the 'sick son of the age' now realized that he was in fact healthy . . . M.'s was henceforth the voice of an outsider who knew he was alone and prized his isolation. M. had come of age and assumed the voice of a witness. His spirit was no longer troubled.

One senses that for her the achievement of this role sets the crown upon the lifetime of artistic effort.

In a way, her memoirs constitute two autobiographies and she has written a more explicit one for Osip than he could have written himself. Mandelstam's metamorphic excitements, his need to perform war-dances in the middle of the war – this would certainly have produced something astonishing, but something less particularized and indexed. He would not have dealt the cards face-up on the table as Nadezhda has done: in his hands they would have become as fluent as the whole spread flowering in the hands of a card-sharp. It is not that his intellectual stamina or moral insight were any less than his wife's but purely a matter of a differently organized response. Mandelstam was interested in the human being as an instrument, how he was framed and tuned: his wife was more interested in the way the instrument was worked upon by the moral intelligence.

As a writer, Nadezhda possesses a quality of tenaciousness, a ledger-maker's appetite for entering everything, making a record as unremitting as it is unadorned. The details remain literal and clear as rivets brightened by the punch: the uneaten egg that had been borrowed as a treat for Akhmatova only to sit on the table all night during a search of the apartment; the marks that Stalin's greasy fingers left on books he was lent; the deadly courteous gesture of Mandelstam's first interrogator: 'I had now nearly sinned against time-honoured tradition by shaking hands with a member of the secret police. But the interrogator saved me from disgrace by not responding – he did not shake hands with people like me – that is, with his potential victims.' One can imagine Osip, in the circumstances, making a metaphor of the man's nature from the way he pronounced a certain word.

As a result of their different gifts and their heroic lives, when Osip died in December 1938 and Nadezhda died in December 1980, nothing died with them. Their achievements have added immeasurably to that 'world culture' which they longed for, and their biographies constitute another tragic instance of what T. S. Eliot perceived as that 'condition of complete simplicity, costing not less than everything'.

[*II*]

The Government of the Tongue

Reading T. S. Eliot and reading about T. S. Eliot were equally formative experiences for my generation. One of the books about him which greatly appealed to me when I first read it in the 1960s was *The New Poetic* by the New Zealand poet and critic, C. K. Stead. The title referred to that movement, critical and creative, which was instituted in the late nineteenth century against discursive poetry, and which Stead judged to have culminated in England with the publication of *The Waste Land* in 1922. One of his purposes was to show how in *The Waste Land* Eliot made a complete break with those popular poets of the day whom Eliot's contemporary, the Russian poet Osip Mandelstam, would have called 'the purveyors of ready-made meaning' – bluff expositors in verse of arguments or narratives which could have been as well conducted in prose. Stead also provided instruction and delight by sussing out titles and reviews of books which 'the new poetry' was up against: such as Anna Bunston's *Songs of God and Man*, perceived by the literary pages to have 'freshness and spirituality'; Augusta Hancock's *Dainty Verses for Little Folk* which were 'written in the right spirit'; and Edwin Drew's *The Chief Incidents in the Titanic Wreck*, which 'may appeal to those who lost relatives in this appalling catastrophe'. These popular volumes (of February 1913) were possessed of a strong horsepower of common-sense meaning. The verse was a metrical piston designed to hammer sentiment or argument into the public ear. This was poetry that made sense, and compared to its candour and decent comprehensibility, *The Waste Land* showed up as a bewildering aberration. In fact, Eliot's poem was hardly available enough to the average reader even to be perceived as an aberration.

Stead also pointed out that the poem was therefore defended or promoted in terms of the public's expectations. Its first defenders argued that if poetry was discourse that made sense, then *The Waste Land* was indeed discourse, except that bits of it were missing. Wrong, Stead averred. This poem 'cannot be seen accurately if it is read as a discourse from which certain "links in the chain" have been omitted'. 'No critic concerned primarily with "meaning" could touch the true "being" of the early poetry.'

The Waste Land in Stead's reading is the vindication of a poetry of image, texture and suggestiveness; of inspiration; of poetry which writes itself. It represents a defeat of the will, an emergence of the ungainsayable and symbolically radiant out of the subconscious deeps. Rational structure has been overtaken or gone through like a sound barrier. The poem does not disdain intellect, yet poetry, having to do with feelings and emotions, must not submit to the intellect's eagerness to foreclose. It must wait for a music to occur, an image to discover itself. Stead thus rehabilitated Eliot as a Romantic poet, every bit as faithful to the process of dream and as susceptible to gifts of the unconscious as Coleridge was before he received the person from Porlock. And so the figure of Old Possum, netted for years in skeins of finely drawn commentary upon his sources, his ideas, his criticism of the modern world and so on, this figure was helped to rise again like Gulliver in Lilliput, no longer a hazy contour of philosophy and literary allusion, but a living principle, a far more natural force than had been recognized until then.

When I thought of 'the government of the tongue' as a general title for these lectures, what I had in mind was this aspect of poetry as its own vindicating force. In this dispensation, the tongue (representing both a poet's personal gift of utterance and the common resources of language itself) has been granted the right to govern. The poetic art is credited with an authority of its own. As readers, we submit to the jurisdiction of achieved form, even though that form is achieved not by dint of the moral and ethical exercise of mind but by the self-validating operations of what we call inspiration – especially if we think of inspiration in the terms supplied by the Polish poet

Anna Swir, who writes of it as a 'psychosomatic phenomenon' and goes on to declare:

> This seems to me the only biologically natural way for a poem to be born and gives the poem something like a biological right to exist. A poet becomes then an antenna capturing the voices of the world, a medium expressing his own subconscious and the collective subconscious. For one moment he possesses wealth usually inaccessible to him, and he loses it when that moment is over.

Poetry's special status among the literary arts derives from the audience's readiness to concede to it a similar efficacy and resource. The poet is credited with a power to open unexpected and unedited communications between our nature and the nature of the reality we inhabit.

The oldest evidence for this attitude appears in the Greek notion that when a lyric poet gives voice, 'it is a god that speaks'. And the attitude persists into the twentieth century: one thinks of Rilke's restatement of it in his *Sonnets to Orpheus* and, in English, we may cite the familiar instance of Robert Frost's essay, 'The Figure a Poem Makes'. For Frost, any interference by the knowing intellect in the purely disinterested cognitions of the form-seeking imagination constitutes poetic sabotage, an affront to the legislative and executive powers of expression itself. 'Read it a hundred times,' he says of the true poem. 'It can never lose its sense of a meaning that once unfolded by surprise as it went.' 'It begins in delight, it inclines to the impulse, it assumes direction with the first line laid down, it runs a course of lucky events and ends in a clarification of life – not necessarily a great clarification, such as sects and cults are founded on, but in a momentary stay against confusion.'

In this figure of the poem's making, then, we see also a paradigm of free action issuing in satisfactorily achieved ends; we see a path projected to the dimension in which, Yeats says, 'Labour is blossoming or dancing where/ The Body is not bruised to pleasure soul'. And just as the poem, in the process of its own genesis, exemplifies a congruence between impulse and right action, so in its repose the poem gives us a premonition of harmonies desired and not inexpensively achieved. In this way, the order of art becomes an achievement intimating a possible order beyond itself, although its relation to that further order remains promissory rather than obligatory. Art is not an inferior reflection of some ordained heavenly system but a rehearsal of it in earthly terms; art does not trace the given map of a better reality but improvises an inspired sketch of it.

My favourite instance of this revision of the Platonic schema is Osip Mandelstam's astonishing fantasia on poetic creation, entitled – since Dante was the pretext for the thing – 'A Conversation about Dante'. A traditional approach to Dante, naturally enough, might involve some attention to the logical, theological and numerological significances which devolve from the number 3, there being three Persons in the Holy Trinity, three lines in each stanza of *The Divine Comedy*, three books in the whole poem, thirty-three cantos in each book, and a rhyme scheme called *terza rima*. All this can press upon the mind until Dante is gradually conceived of as some kind of immense scholastic computer, programmed by Aquinas, and printing out the triadic goods in response to whatever philosophical, metrical and arithmetical data it has been fed. Dante, in other words, is often studied as the great example of a poet whose tongue is governed by an orthodoxy or system, whose free expressiveness is under the strict control of a universe of rules, from the rules of metre to the commandments of the church. Now, enter Mandelstam. Nothing, he implies, could be further from the truth. The three-edged stanza is formed from within, like a crystal, not cut on the outside like a stone. The poem is not governed by external conventions and impositions but follows the laws of its own need. Its composition had all the spontaneity of a chain reaction, of an event in nature:

> We must try to imagine, therefore, how bees might have worked at this thirteen-thousand-faceted form, bees endowed with the brilliant stereometric instinct, who attracted bees in greater and greater numbers as they were required . . . Their cooperation expands and grows more complicated as they participate in the process of forming

the combs, by means of which space virtually emerges out of itself.

This is extraordinarily alive and persuasive, one felicity in a work of disconcertingly abundant genius, the greatest paean I know to the power which poetic imagination wields. Indeed the tongue, which I have been employing here as a synecdoche for that same power, is analogous in this context to the conductor's baton as it is reimagined by Mandelstam. His *hommage* to the baton is too long to quote in full, but this extract should suffice to show how deeply structured in all our thinking is this idea of imagination as a shaping spirit which it is wrong to disobey:

> Which comes first, listening or conducting? If conducting is no more than the nudging along of music which rolls forth of its own accord, then of what use is it when the orchestra is good in itself, when it performs impeccably in itself? . . . This baton is far from being an external, administrative accessory or a distinctive symphonic police which could be done away with within an ideal state. It is no less than a dancing chemical formula which integrates reactions perceptible to the ear. I beg of you not to regard it merely as a supplementary mute instrument, invented for greater visibility and to provide additional pleasure. In a certain sense this invulnerable baton contains within itself all the elements in the orchestra.

As ever, Mandelstam writes jubilantly and persuasively. Far from being perceived as the mouthpiece of an orthodoxy, Dante becomes for him the epitome of chemical suddenness, free biological play, a hive of bees, a hurry of pigeon flights, a flying machine whose function is to keep releasing other self-reproducing flying machines, even, in one manic extended simile, the figure of a Chinese fugitive escaping by leaping from junk to junk across a river crammed with junks, all moving in opposite directions. Dante is thus recanonized as the sponsor of impulse and instinct – not an allegory-framer up to his old didactic tricks in the middle of the journey, but a lyric woodcutter singing in the dark wood of the larynx. Mandelstam brings Dante back from the pantheon to the palate, subverts the age-old impression that his work was written on official paper, and locates his authority not in his cultural representativeness, his religious vision or his sternly unremitting morality but rather in his status as an exemplar of the purely creative, intimate, experimental act of poetry itself.

All the same, as I warm to this theme, a voice from another part of me speaks in rebuke. 'Govern your tongue,' it says, compelling me to remember that my title can also imply a *denial* of the tongue's autonomy and permission. In this reading, 'the government of the tongue' is full of monastic and ascetic strictness. One remembers Hopkins's 'Habit of Perfection', with its command to the eyes to be 'shelled', the ears to attend to silence and the tongue to know its place:

> Shape nothing, lips; be lovely-dumb:
> It is the shut, the curfew sent
> From there where all surrenders come
> Which only makes you eloquent.

It is even more instructive to remember that Hopkins abandoned poetry when he entered the Jesuits, 'as not having to do with my vocation'. This manifests a world where the prevalent values and necessities leave poetry in a relatively underprivileged situation, requiring it to take a position that is secondary to religious truth or state security or public order. It discloses a condition of public and private repressions where the undirected hedonistic play of imagination is regarded at best as luxury or licentiousness, at worst as heresy or treason. In ideal republics, Soviet republics, in the Vatican and Bible-belt, it is a common expectation that the writer will sign over his or her individual, venturesome and potentially disruptive activity into the keeping of an official doctrine, a traditional system, a party line, whatever. In such contexts, no further elaboration or exploration of the language or forms currently in place is permissible. An order has been handed down and the shape of things has been established.

We have grown familiar with the tragic destiny which these circumstances impose upon poets and with the way in which 'ungoverned' poetry and poets, in extreme totalitarian conditions, can become a form of alternative government, or government in exile. I was struck, for example, to learn that lines by the poet Czeslaw Milosz are incorporated into the memorial to the Solidarity workers outside the gates of the Lenin Shipyard in Gdansk. But I was stunned by the image which Andrei Sinyavsky provides of the subversive and necessary function of writing as truth-telling, when he tells how, at the height of the Stalin terror, Alexander Kutzenov used to seal his manuscripts in glass preserving jars and bury them in his garden at night-time. It is all there, the suggestion of art's curative powers, its stored goodness and its ultimate appeal to 'the reader in posterity'. The scene has the perturbing oneiric reality of an actual dream and could stand for the kind of ominous premonition which a dictator might experience, waking in the small hours and remembering the reality of the poetry he would constrain.

For the moment, however, I am concerned with states of affairs less repressive and less malign. I am thinking not so much of authoritarian censorship as of an implacable consensus in which the acceptable themes are given variously resourceful treatments, and in which the felicity or correctness of a work's execution constitutes the conspicuous focus of attention for both audience and artist. It is not right to assume that such conditions always produce inferior art. As a poet, for example, George Herbert surrendered himself to a framework of belief and an instituted religion; but in his case, it happened that his personality was structured in such a way that he could dwell in amity with doctrine, writing a poetry which was intellectually pure, emotionally robust and entirely authentic. An unconstrained, undebilitated mind measured itself against impositions and expectations which were both fundamental and contingent to it. Its discipline, however, proved equal to its challenges, so that a pun on the word *choler*, meaning both outburst of anger and emblem of submission, could hold the psychic and artistic balance; and a rhyme of 'child' with 'wild' could put the distress of his personal predicament in a divinely ordained perspective.

Moreover, what holds for George Herbert also holds for the T. S. Eliot who wrote *Four Quartets*. As C. K. Stead also pointed out, this was a poet very different from the one who wrote *The Waste Land*, one who turned from an earlier trust in process and image to embrace the claims of argument and idea. To this grave and senior figure, the example of Dante was also important, although his import was significantly different for Eliot than for Mandelstam. Both men, interestingly enough, were turning to the great Florentine at a moment of mid-life crisis, Eliot's first essay appearing in 1929 and Mandelstam's being written, though not published, in the early 1930s. (One thinks again of preserving jars in the dark garden.) Mandelstam was interested primarily in vindication by language, Eliot in salvation by conversion. Eliot's essay ends with an evocation of the world of the *Vita Nuova*, of the necessary attempt to enter it, an attempt 'as difficult and hard as rebirth', and bows out with the declaration that 'there is almost a definite moment of acceptance when the New Life begins'. Here, ten years before the *Quartets* began in earnest, Eliot's writing looks forward to the concerns of those poems. What obsessed Mandelstam and shook him into heady critical song – namely, the sensuous foragings and transports of the body of poetic language – hardly seems to interest Eliot at all. He is much more preoccupied with the philosophical and religious significances which can be drawn from a work of art, its truth quotient rather than its technique/beauty quotient, its aura of cultural and spiritual force. There is a stern and didactic profile to the Dante whom Eliot conjures up and, as he embraces a religious faith, it is to this profile he would submit in order that it be re-created in his own work.

The Eliot of *The Waste Land*, on the other hand, reproduced in his poem a sense of bewilderment and somnambulism, a flow of inventive expressionist scenes reminiscent of those which Virgil and Dante encounter in *The Divine Comedy*. In the *Inferno*, pilgrim and guide proceed among shades in thrall to the fates of which they have become the archetypes, in much the same way as Eliot's poem proceeds upon the eerie flood of its own inventiveness. But in the *Quartets*, Eliot has been born again out of the romance of symbolism into the stricter exactions of *philosophia* and religious tradition. The inspired, spontaneous, essentially lyric tongue has been replaced as governor by an organ that functions more like a sorrowful *grand seigneur*, meditatively, authoritatively, yet just a little wistfully aware of its lost vitality and insouciance.

That vitality and insouciance of lyric poetry, its relish of its own inventiveness, its pleasuring strain, always comes under threat when poetry remembers that its self-gratification must be perceived as a kind of affront to a world preoccupied with its own imperfections, pains and catastrophes. What right has poetry to its quarantine? Should it not put the governors on its joy and moralize its song? Should it, as Austin Clarke said in another context, take the clapper from the bell of rhyme? Should it go as far in self-denial as Zbigniew Herbert's poem 'A Knocker' seems to want it to go? This translation, in the Penguin Modern European Poets series, was originally published in 1968:

> There are those who grow
> gardens in their heads
> paths lead from their hair
> to sunny and white cities
>
> it's easy for them to write
> they close their eyes
> immediately schools of images
> stream down their foreheads
>
> my imagination
> is a piece of board
> my sole instrument
> is a wooden stick
>
> I strike the board
> it answers me
> yes – yes
> no – no
>
> for others the green bell of a tree
> the blue bell of water
> I have a knocker
> from unprotected gardens

[99]

I thump on the board
and it prompts me
with the moralist's dry poem
yes – yes
no – no

Herbert's poem ostensibly demands that poetry abandon its hedonism and fluency, that it become a nun of language and barber its luxuriant locks down to a stubble of moral and ethical goads. Ostensibly too, it would depose the tongue because of its cavalier indulgence and send in as governor of the estate of poetry a Malvolio with a stick. It would castigate the entrancements of poetry, substituting in their stead a roundhead's plain-spoken counsel. Yet oddly, without the fluent evocation of bells and gardens and trees and all those things which it explicitly deplores, the poem could not make the bleak knocker signify as potently as it does. The poem makes us feel that we should prefer moral utterance to palliative imagery, but it does exactly that, makes us *feel*, and by means of feeling carries truth alive into the heart – exactly as the Romantics said it should. We end up persuaded we are against lyric poetry's culpable absorption in its own process by an entirely successful instance of that very process in action: here is a lyric about a knocker which claims that lyric is inadmissible.

All poets who get beyond the first excitement of being blessed by the achievement of poetic form confront, sooner or later, the question which Herbert confronts in 'A Knocker' and, if they are lucky, they end up, like Herbert, outstripping it rather than answering it directly. Some, like Wilfred Owen, outface it by living a life so extremely mortgaged to the suffering of others that the tenancy of the palace of art is paid for a hundredfold. Others, like Yeats, promulgate and practise such faith in art's absolutely absolved necessity that they overbear whatever assaults the historical and contingent might mount upon their certitude. Richard Ellmann's statement of the Yeatsian case is finally applicable to every serious poetic life:

He wishes to show how brute force may be transmogrified, how we can sacrifice ourselves . . . to our 'imagined' selves which offer far higher standards than anything

offered by social convention. If we must suffer, it is better
to create the world in which we suffer, and this is what
heroes do spontaneously, artists do consciously, and all
men do in their degree.

Every poet does indeed proceed upon some such conviction,
even those who are most scrupulous in their avoidance of the
grand manner, who respect the democracy of language, and
display by the pitch of their voice or the commonness of their
subjects a readiness to put themselves on the side of those who
are sceptical of poetry's right to any special status. The fact is
that poetry is its own reality and no matter how much a poet
may concede to the corrective pressures of social, moral,
political and historical reality, the ultimate fidelity must be to
the demands and promise of the artistic event.

It is for this reason that I want to discuss 'At the Fishhouses'
by Elizabeth Bishop. Here we see this most reticent and
mannerly of poets being compelled by the undeniable impetus
of her art to break with her usual inclination to conciliate the
social audience. This conciliatory impulse was not based on
subservience but on a respect for other people's shyness in the
face of poetry's presumption: she usually limited herself to a
note that would not have disturbed the discreet undersong of
conversation between strangers breakfasting at a seaside hotel.
Without addressing a question as immense and unavoidable as
whether silence rather than poetry is not the proper response in
a world after Auschwitz, she implicitly condones the doubts
about art's prerogatives which such a question raises.

Elizabeth Bishop, in other words, was temperamentally
inclined to believe in the government of the tongue – in the self-
denying sense. She was personally reticent, opposed to and
incapable of self-aggrandizement, the very embodiment of
good manners. Manners, of course, imply obligations to others
and obligations on the part of others to ourselves. They insist
on propriety, in the good large original sense of the word,
meaning that which is intrinsic and characteristic and belongs
naturally to the person or the thing. They also imply a certain
strictness and allow the verbs 'ought' and 'should' to come into
play. In short, as an attribute of the poetic enterprise, manners

place limits on the whole scope and pitch of the enterprise itself. They would govern the tongue.

But Elizabeth Bishop not only practised good manners in her poetry. She also submitted herself to the discipline of observation. Observation was her habit, as much in the monastic, Hopkinsian sense as in its commoner meaning of a customarily repeated action. Indeed, observation is itself a manifestation of obedience, an activity which is averse to overwhelming phenomena by the exercise of subjectivity, content to remain an assisting presence rather than an overbearing pressure. So it is no wonder that the title of Bishop's last book was that of an old school textbook, *Geography III*. It is as if she were insisting on an affinity between her poetry and textbook prose, which establishes reliable, unassertive relations with the world by steady attention to detail, by equable classification and level-toned enumeration. The epigraph of the book suggests that the poet wishes to identify with these well-tried, primary methods of connecting words and things:

> *What is geography?*
> A description of the earth's surface.
>
> *What is the earth?*
> The planet or body on which we live.
>
> *What is the shape of the earth?*
> Round, like a ball.
>
> *Of what is the earth's surface composed?*
> Land and water.

A poetry faithful to such catechetical procedures would indeed seem to deny itself access to vision or epiphany; and 'At the Fishhouses' does begin with fastidious notations which log the progress of the physical world, degree by degree, into the world of the poet's own lucid but unemphatic awareness:

> Although it is a cold evening,
> down by one of the fishhouses
> an old man sits netting,
> his net, in the gloaming almost invisible,
> a dark purple-brown,
> and his shuttle worn and polished.

The air smells so strong of codfish
it makes one's nose run and one's eyes water.
The five fishhouses have steeply peaked roofs
and narrow, cleated gangplanks slant up
to storerooms in the gables
for the wheelbarrows to be pushed up and down on.
All is silver: the heavy surface of the sea,
swelling slowly as if considering spilling over,
is opaque, but the silver of the benches,
the lobster pots, and masts, scattered
among the wild jagged rocks,
is of an apparent translucence
like the small old buildings with an emerald moss
growing on their shoreward walls.
The big fish tubs are completely lined
with layers of beautiful herring scales
and the wheelbarrows are similarly plastered
with creamy iridescent coats of mail,
with small iridescent flies crawling on them.
Up on the little slope behind the houses,
set in the sparse bright sprinkle of grass,
is an ancient wooden capstan,
cracked, with two long bleached handles
and some melancholy stains, like dried blood,
where the ironwork has rusted.
The old man accepts a Lucky Strike.
He was a friend of my grandfather.
We talk of the decline in the population
and of codfish and herring
while he waits for a herring boat to come in.
There are sequins on his vest and on his thumb.
He has scraped the scales, the principal beauty,
from unnumbered fish with that black old knife,
the blade of which is almost worn away.

Down at the water's edge, at the place
where they haul up the boats, up the long ramp
descending into the water, thin silver
tree trunks are laid horizontally

across the gray stones, down and down
at intervals of four or five feet.

Cold dark deep and absolutely clear,
element bearable to no mortal,
to fish and to seals . . . One seal particularly
I have seen here evening after evening.
He was curious about me. He was interested in music;
like me a believer in total immersion,
so I used to sing him Baptist hymns.
I also sang 'A Mighty Fortress Is Our God.'
He stood up in the water and regarded me
steadily, moving his head a little.
Then he would disappear, then suddenly emerge
almost in the same spot, with a sort of shrug
as if it were against his better judgment.
Cold dark deep and absolutely clear,
the clear gray icy water . . . Back, behind us,
the dignified tall firs begin.
Bluish, associating with their shadows,
a million Christmas trees stand
waiting for Christmas. The water seems suspended
above the rounded gray and blue-gray stones.
I have seen it over and over, the same sea, the same,
slightly, indifferently swinging above the stones,
icily free above the stones,
above the stones and then the world.
If you should dip your hand in,
your wrist would ache immediately,
your bones would begin to ache and your hand would burn
as if the water were a transmutation of fire
that feeds on stones and burns with a dark gray flame.
If you tasted it, it would first taste bitter,
then briny, then surely burn your tongue.
It is like what we imagine knowledge to be:
dark, salt, clear, moving utterly free,
drawn from the cold hard mouth
of the world, derived from the rocky breasts
forever, flowing and drawn, and since
our knowledge is historical, flowing, and flown.

What we have been offered, among other things, is the slow-motion spectacle of a well-disciplined poetic imagination being tempted to dare a big leap, hesitating, and then with powerful sureness actually taking the leap. For about two-thirds of the poem the restraining, self-abnegating, completely attentive manners of the writing keep us alive to the surfaces of a world: the note is colloquial if tending towards the finical, the scenery is chaste, beloved and ancestral. Grandfather was here. Yet this old world is still being made new again by the sequins of herring scales, the sprinkle of grass and the small iridescent flies. Typically, detail by detail, by the layering of one observation upon another, by readings taken at different levels and from different angles, a world is brought into being. There is a feeling of ordered scrutiny, of a securely positioned observer turning a gaze now to the sea, now to the fish barrels, now to the old man. And the voice that tells us about it all is self-possessed but not self-centred, full of discreet and intelligent instruction, of the desire to witness exactly. The voice is neither breathless nor detached; it is thoroughly plenished, like the sea 'swelling slowly as if considering spilling over', and then, thrillingly, half-way through, it does spill over:

> Cold dark deep and absolutely clear,
> element bearable to no mortal,
> to fish and to seals . . . One seal particularly

Just a minute ago I said that the habit of observation did not promise any irruption of the visionary. Yet here it is, a rhythmic heave which suggests that something other is about to happen – although not immediately. The colloquial note creeps back and the temptation to inspired utterance is rebuked by the seal who arrives partly like a messenger from another world, partly like a dead-pan comedian of water. Even so, he is a sign which initiates a wonder as he dives back into the deep region where the poem will follow, wooed with perfect timing into the mysterious. Looking at the world of the surface, after all, is not only against the better judgement of a seal; it is finally also against the better judgement of the poet.

It is not that the poet breaks faith with the observed world, the world of human attachment, grandfathers, Lucky Strikes and Christmas trees. But it is a different, estranging and fearful element which ultimately fascinates her: the world of meditated meaning, of a knowledge-need which sets human beings apart from seals and herrings, and sets the poet in her solitude apart from her grandfather and the old man, this poet enduring the cold sea-light of her own *wyrd* and her own mortality. Her scientific impulse is suddenly jumped back to its root in pre-Socratic awe, and water stares her in the face as the original solution:

> If you should dip your hand in,
> your wrist would ache immediately,
> your bones would begin to ache and your hand would
>   burn
> as if the water were a transmutation of fire
> that feeds on stones and burns with a dark gray flame.
> If you tasted it, it would first taste bitter,
> then briny, then surely burn your tongue.
> It is like what we imagine knowledge to be:
> dark, salt, clear, moving, utterly free,
> drawn from the cold hard mouth
> of the world, derived from the rocky breasts
> forever, flowing and drawn, and since
> our knowledge is historical, flowing, and flown.

This writing still bears a recognizable resemblance to the simple propositions of the geography text-book. There is no sentence which does not possess a similar clarity and unchallengeability. Yet since these concluding lines are poetry, not geography, they have a dream truth as well as a daylight truth about them, they are as hallucinatory as they are accurate. They also possess that *sine qua non* of all lyric utterance, a completely persuasive inner cadence which is deeply intimate with the laden water of full tide. The lines are inhabited by certain profoundly true tones, which as Robert Frost put it, 'were before words were, living in the cave of the mouth', and they do what poetry most essentially does: they fortify our inclination to credit prompt-ings of our intuitive being. They help us to say in the first recesses of ourselves, in the shyest, pre-social part of our nature, 'Yes, I know something like that too. Yes, that's right; thank you for putting words on it and making it more or less official.' And thus the government of the tongue gains our votes, and Anna Swir's proclamation (which at first may have sounded a bit overstated) comes true in the sensation of reading even a poet as shy of bardic presumption as Elizabeth Bishop:

> A poet becomes then an antenna capturing the voices of the world, a medium expressing his own subconscious and the collective subconscious.

In the three lectures which follow, I shall explore the ways in which W. H. Auden, Robert Lowell and Sylvia Plath each contrived to become 'an antenna'. And in concluding this one, I want now to offer two further 'texts' for meditation. The first is from T. S. Eliot. Forty-four years ago, in October 1942, in wartime London, when he was at work on 'Little Gidding', Eliot wrote in a letter to E. Martin Browne:

> In the midst of what is going on now, it is hard, when you sit down at a desk, to feel confident that morning after morning spent fiddling with words and rhythms is justified activity – especially as there is never any certainty that the whole thing won't have to be scrapped. And on the other hand, external or public activity is more of a drug than is this solitary toil which often seems so pointless.

Here is the great paradox of poetry and of the imaginative arts in general. Faced with the brutality of the historical onslaught, they are practically useless. Yet they verify our singularity, they strike and stake out the ore of self which lies at the base of every individuated life. In one sense the efficacy of poetry is nil – no lyric has ever stopped a tank. In another sense, it is unlimited. It is like the writing in the sand in the face of which accusers and accused are left speechless and renewed.

I am thinking of Jesus' writing as it is recorded in Chapter Eight of John's Gospel, my second and concluding text:

> And the scribes and Pharisees brought unto him a woman taken in adultery; and when they had set her in the midst,

They say unto him, Master, this woman was taken in adultery, in the very act.

Now Moses in the law commanded us, that such should be stoned: but what sayest thou?

This they said, tempting him, that they might have to accuse him. But Jesus stooped down, and with his finger wrote on the ground, as though he heard them not.

So when they continued asking him, he lifted up himself, and said unto them, He that is without sin among you, let him first cast a stone at her.

And again he stooped down, and wrote on the ground.

And they which heard it, being convicted by their own conscience, went out one by one, beginning at the eldest, even unto the last: and Jesus was left alone, and the woman standing in the midst.

When Jesus had lifted up himself, and saw none but the woman, he said unto her, Woman, where are those thine accusers? hath no man condemned thee?

She said, No man, Lord. And Jesus said unto her, Neither do I condemn thee: go, and sin no more.

The drawing of those characters is like poetry, a break with the usual life but not an absconding from it. Poetry, like the writing, is arbitrary and marks time in every possible sense of that phrase. It does not say to the accusing crowd or to the helpless accused, 'Now a solution will take place', it does not propose to be instrumental or effective. Instead, in the rift between what is going to happen and whatever we would wish to happen, poetry holds attention for a space, functions not as distraction but as pure concentration, a focus where our power to concentrate is concentrated back on ourselves.

This is what gives poetry its governing power. At its greatest moments it would attempt, in Yeats's phrase, to hold in a single thought reality and justice. Yet even then its function is not essentially supplicatory or transitive. Poetry is more a threshold than a path, one constantly approached and constantly departed from, at which reader and writer undergo in their different ways the experience of being at the same time summoned and released.

Sounding Auden

What I want to explore in this lecture is the shifting relation between the kind of poetic authority which W. H. Auden sought and achieved and what might be described as his poetic music. By poetic authority I mean the rights and weight which accrue to a voice not only because of a sustained history of truth-telling but by virtue also of its tonality, the sway it gains over the deep ear and, through that, over other parts of our mind and nature. By poetic music I mean the technical means, the more or less describable effects of language and form, by which a certain tonality is effected and maintained. I shall listen in to some passages of Auden's work and try to describe what is to be heard there; I shall also try to follow some of the echoes which the passages set up and ask how these echoes contribute to the poetry's scope or suggest its limitations.

In his prose, Auden constantly returned to the double nature of poetry. On the one hand, poetry could be regarded as magical incantation, fundamentally a matter of sound and the power of sound to bind our minds' and bodies' apprehensions within an acoustic complex; on the other hand, poetry is a matter of making wise and true meanings, of commanding our emotional assent by the intelligent disposition and inquisition of human experience. In fact, most poems – including Auden's – constitute temporary stays against the confusion threatened by the mind's inclination to accept both accounts of poetic function in spite of their potential mutual exclusiveness. But confusion is probably far too strong a word, since Auden is able to make a resolving parable of the duality, assigning the beauty/magic part to Ariel and the truth/meaning part to Prospero and proposing that every poem, indeed every poet, embodies a dialogue between them. Ariel stands for poetry's enchantment, our need to be bewitched: 'We want a poem to be beautiful, that is to say, a verbal earthly paradise, a timeless world of pure play which gives us delight precisely because of its contrast to our historical existence.' This want, of course, if fully indulged, would lead poetry into self-deception and hence the countervailing presence of Prospero, whose covenant is with 'truth' rather than 'beauty' – 'and a poet cannot bring us any truth without introducing into his poetry the problematic, the painful, the disorderly, the ugly'.

All this is self-evident. Yet how we answer questions about the value of Auden's poetry will have to do with the relative values we attach to poetic sense and poetic sound: it will have to do with the way we answer the question which Auden himself posed in his delightful short poem 'Orpheus': 'What does the song hope for . . . To be bewildered and happy,/ Or most of all the knowledge of life?' Auden's own unsatisfactory resolution of a similar crux, his famous revision of *or* to *and* in the line 'We must love one another or die', may suggest a quick answer at the outset: song hopes to be happy *and* to possess the knowledge of life. But to come so quickly to so glib a conclusion would rob us of the pleasure of inquiring into the fabric of the poetry itself.

Hard-bitten, aggressively up to date in the way it took cognizance of the fallen contemporary landscape, yet susceptible also to the pristine scenery of an imaginary Anglo-Saxon England, Auden's original voice could not have been predicted and was utterly timely. In the late 1920s and early 1930s, he caught native English poetry by the scruff of the neck, pushed its nose sharply into modernity, made it judder and frolic from the shock over the course of a decade, and then allowed it to resume a more amiable relation with its comfortably domestic inheritance. His opus represents in the end what his insights insisted upon in the beginning: the necessity of a break, of an escape from habit, an escape from the given; and he insists upon the necessity of these acts of self-liberation only to expose their ultimately illusory promise.

Correspondingly, his career represents the full turn of the wheel from his initial rejection of a milieu and a tradition to his

final complaisant incorporation within them. It is as if, like
Tiresias, he foresuffers all and yet, for all that he knows, knows
that he will find neither escape nor completion. Or perhaps one
should say instead that he will find neither forgiveness nor
salvation – things which can be found only by setting historical
time in relation to another eternal life that looks over the
shoulder of history itself:

> She looked over his shoulder
>   For vines and olive trees,
> Marble well-governed cities
>   And ships upon untamed seas
> But there on the shining metal
>   His hands had put instead
> An artificial wilderness
>   And a sky like lead.

This is the goddess Thetis at the shoulder of the thin-lipped
armourer, Hephaestos, and the poem it comes from, 'The
Shield of Achilles', represents Auden in his composed, equably
mature poetic years, taking the long sad universal view of
historical cycles. The melodious note of those lines and their
impassiveness are the result of the kind of synoptic wisdom
which this poet settled into and settled for. But I wish to begin
with a much earlier poem which he eventually entitled 'Venus
Will Now Say a Few Words'. Here Venus stands for the gate
and goad of life, the sexual constant and eternal drive. She – or
it – addresses an unspecified subject who is characteristically
on the verge of what he hopes will be significant action. And, as
usual, his choice and crisis and action are perceived to be as
necessary as they are undesired:

> Your shutting up the house and taking prow
> To go into the wilderness to pray,
> Means that I wish to leave and to pass on,
> Select another form, perhaps your son;
> Though he reject you, join opposing team
> Be late or early at another time,
> My treatment will not differ – he will be tipped,
> Found weeping, signed for, made to answer, topped.

> Do not imagine you can abdicate;
> Before you reach the frontier you are caught;
> Others have tried it and will try again
> To finish that which they did not begin:
> Their fate must always be the same as yours,
> To suffer the loss they were afraid of, yes,
> Holders of one position, wrong for years.

This has the young Auden's typical combination of doomwatch and kicking energy. The voice of the inevitable is speaking, the voice of evolutionary force, the voice of what he would eventually and notoriously, in the last stanza of 'Spain', call History. So it is proper that the poem should move with piston-fired inevitability and that its driving force should be generated by the couplet, that little pile-driver among the metres, banging, knocking, butting, beating time. And it is also proper that the poem should sound incapable of 'help or pardon', those palliatives which History, in the crucial stanza written eight years later, would still be unable to extend to the defeated. There, however, History was going to be allowed to say *Alas*, and while the message in the lines quoted above may indeed be unpardoning, the voice is kept from going over the top into punitiveness or vindictiveness by Auden's muffling the drum of rhyme:

> Their fate must always be the same as yours,
> To suffer the loss they were afraid of, yes,
> Holders of one position, wrong for years.

Pararhyme, Wilfred Owen's technically simple but emotionally complicating innovation, had been applied by Owen most systematically in the poem 'Strange Meeting' which dramatized an encounter between doubles and lamented the collapse of trust in progress and all such melioristic notions. Owen had further declared that 'All a poet can do today is warn'. So, poetically and historically, it is proper that Auden's poem of admonition should also employ pararhyme and thereby echo the earlier one.

The verse lines, therefore, reach like sounding lines down to the mud of Flanders, back to that 'conscientious objector with a

very seared conscience'. Owen's joining up, his training of
recruits to kill and be killed, the terrible strain which he inflicted
on himself by maintaining a patriotic courage in face of personal
revulsion and trauma – all this did not release him from the
recognition that nothing would be improved by his sacrifice.
This too made Owen a true precursor of the Auden of 'Spain',
the poet who connived in what he deplored, that which he
would at first call 'the necessary murder' and then, in a more
generally lenient revision, 'the fact of murder'.

Owen must have been in Auden's mind, if only as a technical
exemplar. But I want to keep sounding things, perhaps beyond
due measure, and to go further back. The reference in the lines
quoted to the topping – that is, the hanging – of a son recalled
to me Walter Ralegh's sonnet to *his* son, his wag, his pretty
knave; and to remember Ralegh's lines, written also under the
shadow of public danger, is to gain a new perspective on
Auden. Ralegh's poem is tender and morbid, haunted by a
suppressed conviction that what it presents as a merry if
minatory fancy has indeed the status of an awful prophetic
dream. The surface noise is cheery but its background music is a
dolorous, steady roll of tumbril wheels:

> Three things there be that prosper up apace
> And flourish, whilst they grow asunder far;
> But on a day, they meet all in one place,
> And when they meet, they one another mar.
> And they be these: the wood, the weed, the wag.
> The wood is that which makes the gallow tree;
> The weed is that which strings the hangman's bag;
> The wag, my pretty knave, betokeneth thee.
> Mark well, dear boy, while these assemble not,
> Green springs the tree, hemp grows, the wag is wild;
> But when they meet, it makes the timber rot,
> It frets the halter, and it chokes the child.
> Then bless thee, and beware, and let us pray
> We part not with thee at this meeting day.

Long before the unconscious forced itself into language as a
Freudian concept, it was playing like St Elmo's fire round the
lines of a poem such as this. The crucial difference, of course,

between Auden's canvassing of the hanged-son image and Ralegh's poetic compulsion to it lies in just this division between pre-Freudian and post-Freudian awareness; and while Auden gains in poetic strategy because of the advance, he does lose somewhat in poetic energy. Where Ralegh's vision of the dreadful rises like a ballad woodcut from the folk imagination, bearing an aura of *déjà vu* and the uncanny, Auden's feels more like the result of consulting an index of motifs. The rat-a-tat-tat of Auden's poem's movement, the half-donnish expectation that we will pick up an allusion to Horace's fugitive changing the skies but not his fate as he hastens overseas, the talk about an 'opposing team' within a context that pretends to the oracular, the gradual accession of a fast tone over a solemn occasion, all this comes from Auden's strategic intelligence being just that little bit too much in control of things.

What is in evidence here is his ambition to write a new kind of English poem with what he described in his poem to Christopher Isherwood as a 'strict and adult pen'. Elaborating on this, in his introduction to his book *The Auden Generation*, Samuel Hynes characterizes the sought-after new art as follows:

> Auden was urging a kind of writing that would be affective, immediate, concerned with ideas, moral not aesthetic in its central intention, and organized by that intention rather than by its correspondence to the observed world. The problem he posed was not simply a formal one – finding an alternate way of writing a Georgian lyric or a realistic novel – but something more difficult: he was asking for alternative *worlds*, worlds of the imagination which would consist of new, significant forms, and through which literature could play a moral role in a time of crisis.

This is well said and could apply to another poem which I also want to place in alignment with 'Venus Will Now Say a Few Words', in order to search out what remains ultimately unsatisfactory about Auden's poem. Hynes could be describing work that would be done a couple of decades later than Auden by the historically tested imaginations of post-war poets in Eastern Europe; and indeed the poem we have been lingering over belongs to a genre which was fully developed only after the trauma of the Nazi experience. Auden's genius sketched out the possibilities but it was the fate of the Poles and Czechs and Hungarians to bring it fully into literary service. The kind of work I am thinking of is represented by Czeslaw Milosz's 'Child of Europe', of which this is Section IV:

Grow your tree of falsehood from a small grain of truth.
Do not follow those who lie in contempt of reality.

Let your lie be even more logical than the truth itself.
So the weary travellers may find repose in the lie.

After the Day of the Lie gather in select circles,
Shaking with laughter when our real deeds are mentioned.

Dispensing flattery called: perspicacious thinking.
Dispensing flattery called: a great talent.

We, the last who can still draw joy from cynicism,
We, whose cunning is not unlike despair.

A new humourless generation is now arising.
It takes in deadly earnest all we received with deadly laughter.

What distinguishes Milosz's poem is its groundswell of complete certitude about the shape of things. Even though this is a translation, I am convinced that we are getting something true to the original Polish because here, to rephrase Wilfred Owen, the poetry is in the plotting. Or, to go back to one of the terms I used at the start of the lecture, the poetry makes true meanings and commands our emotional assent by the intelligent disposition and inquisition of human experience.

'Child of Europe' is both historical and parabolic, it has gone far past the simplicity of confession and its reticence is that of the morning after savagery. It is the cry of a moral creature being racked by the turn which history is taking in Europe of the 1940s, and equally it is a psychic model, sprung from a source somewhere between nightmare and haughtiness, every bit as much as an apparition out of the personal depths as Ralegh's prophetic frisson. Which is another way of saying that its reach in is as long as its reach out, that it is equally efficacious as satire or self-scrutiny. Compared with it, Auden's lines are in the dock for cleverness, although to say so is to be unfair to the poet who had broken through at this time with a kind of poem which carried the English lyric well beyond the domestic securities of the first person singular. Carried it, in fact, towards that kind of impersonal, eschatological poetry of post-war Europe of which contemporary English poetry is just now beginning to take proper cognizance.

From the start, Auden's imagination was eager to make a connection between the big picture that was happening outside in Europe and England and the small one which was being shown inside himself: he sensed the crisis in a public world poised for renewal or catastrophe as analogous to an impending private crisis of action and choice in his own life. Poets with a firmed-up sense of themselves and their art had reacted in the past to such counterbalancing pressures in a variety of ways: with therapeutic autobiographical essays like *The Prelude* or *In Memoriam*; with meditative lament, like 'Dover Beach'; with a projection of the self's revolutionary glamour in 'Ode to the West Wind', or a parade of its patrician autonomy in *The Tower*. But all of this work came from poets with already established habits of address, and footholds in a social and literary landscape which they could regard as more or less stable.

Meanwhile of course, in conditions where the ground might open under the present, a newer approach which Eliot had dubbed 'the mythical method' had become available. This was the art of holding a classical safety net under the tottering data of the contemporary, of paralleling, shadowing, archetypifying – the art practised in *Ulysses* and *The Waste Land* and the early sections of Pound's *Cantos*. This was more like what Auden needed, yet Auden, unlike the masters who produced these works, was neither expatriate nor antagonist; he was English, in place, and aching for relation. Consequently, he had more fidelity to the traditional modes of English poetry than the first modernists had, was less eclectic in his literary tastes and sources, and much more at home in a domestic English landscape and history. He did, however, have a strong intuition of the unreliability of the shelter which all of this offered and while he naturally cherished it, he had a strong urge to divest himself of it.

He was hungering for a form. In his unformed needs and impulses he was rehearsing the scenario which Martin Buber outlines in *I and Thou* as follows:

> This is the eternal source of art: a man is faced by a form which desires to be made through him into a work. This form is no offspring of his soul but is an appearance which steps up to it and demands of it the effective power. The man is concerned with an act of his being. If he carries it through, if he speaks the primary word out of his being to the form which appears, then the effective power streams out, and the work arises.

That is actually a firm account of what in experience is elusive and tenebrous; and in its conception of power streaming out and the work arising as the primary word is spoken, it represents a way of acknowledging the kind of governing power to which the young Auden's tongue gained access when acts of his being issued in his own words, those entirely compelling, if estranged and estranging words of his famous earliest poems.

This new lyric was dominated by a somewhat impersonal pronoun which enclosed much that was fabulous, passional and occasionally obscure. Its manifestations were an 'I', or 'we' or 'you' which could arrest, confuse and inspect the reader all at once. He or she seemed to have been set down in the middle of a cold landscape, blindfolded, turned rapidly around, unblind-folded, ordered to march and to make sense of every ominous thing encountered from there on. The new poem turned the reader into an accomplice, unaccountably bound to the poem's presiding voice by an insinuation that they shared a knowledge which might be either shameful or subversive. In Hynes's terms, it presented an alternative world. Even Eliot's openings, startling as they were, could not equal Auden's for defamiliariz-ing abruptness. Eliot still pushed the poem out with the current of rhythmic expectation, the words sailed off relatively unhampered towards attainable syntactical or scenic or narra-tive destinations.

Let us go then, you and I,
When the evening is spread out against the sky . . .

> *All right, then. Let's go.*

April is the cruellest month, breeding
Lilacs out of the dead land, mixing
Memory and desire, stirring . . .

> *OK. Keep talking. What else*
> *was bothering you?*

Here I am, an old man in a dry month
Being read to by a boy, waiting for rain.

> *Sure, granpa! Of course you are.*

Auden's openings, on the other hand, were launched against a
flow. The craft itself felt shipshape, but its motion seemed
unpredictable, it started in mid-pitch and wobbled:

Who stands, the crux left of the watershed,
On the wet road between the chafing grass . . .

> *Between grass? What do you*
> *mean? Where is this anyway?*

Taller to-day, we remember similar evenings,
Walking together in the windless orchard . . .

> *Taller what? Whose orchard*
> *where?*

These famous early poems gave me enormous trouble when I
was an undergraduate. Confident teachers spoke of Geoffrey
Grigson's advice to Thirties poets to 'Report well. Begin with
objects and events.' These poets were socially concerned, we
were told; they were tempted by communism, wanted to open
some negotiation with popular culture, and to include the
furniture of the modern technological world in their lyrics.
Fine. This was OK for the nude giant girls behind Spender's
pylons and the knockabout farce of Louis MacNeice's 'Bagpipe

Music'. But Auden was supposed to be the main man, so where
did all this lecture-note stuff get you when in the solitude of
your room you faced the staccato imperatives of a passage like
this:

> Go home, now, stranger, proud of your young stock,
> Stranger, turn back again, frustrate and vexed:
> This land, cut off, will not communicate,
> Be no accessory content to one
> Aimless for faces rather there than here.
> Beams from your car may cross a bedroom wall,
> They wake no sleeper; you may hear the wind
> Arriving driven from the ignorant sea
> To hurt itself on pane, on bark of elm
> Where sap unbaffled rises, being spring;
> But seldom this. Near you, taller than grass,
> Ears poise before decision, scenting danger.

My teachers had used the word 'telegraphese', so I assumed I
was in its presence here, the enigma and abruptness of the
thing suggesting as much the actual chattering of a machine
relaying signals as the condensed idiom of a decoded, printed
message. So, all right, telegraphese. Yet to what end? I felt
excluded. I had indeed been blindfolded and turned around
only to find myself daunted by a landscape that both convinced
me and shrugged me off.

It would have been better had those teachers been in a
position to quote what Geoffrey Grigson wrote four decades
later, in the volume of memorial tributes edited by Stephen
Spender. There, talking about the first poem of Auden's which
he had encountered, one never to be republished, Grigson
spoke of its having arisen out of an 'Englishness' until then
unexpressed or not isolated in a poem.

> In the poem, he [Auden] saw the blood trail which had
> dripped from Grendel after his arm and shoulder had
> been ripped off by Beowulf. The blood shone, was
> phosphorescent on the grass . . . It was as if Auden . . .
> had given imaginative place and 'reality' to something

exploited for the Examination Schools, yet rooted in the English origins.

Grigson also spoke of 'assonances and alliterations coming together to make a new verbal actuality as it might be of rock or quartz', which is precisely what this slab of verse felt like to me when I first encountered it, and why I still rejoice in it. It is responses and formulations such as Grigson's, which have little to say about the young poet's shifting allegiances to Marx and Freud, that are the ones which count for most in the long poetic run, because they are the most intrinsically sensitive to the art of language.

Much has been written about the ideological and theological strenuousness within this poet's career. Much commentary has been generated by his subsequent revision or excision from the canon of his work of many explicitly political and hortatory utterances made during the time of his most ardent address to public themes. Less appears to have got said about that 'poetic music' to which I referred in the beginning, and to which Grigson is here particularly sensitive. Impressionistic and text-centred as such criticism may be, it still has a place in verifying the reality of poetry in the world. It may not be as up to date in its idiom as that found in some recent Auden commentators, such as Stan Smith, whose deconstructionist tools yield many excellent insights: Smith maintains that early Auden, for example, is both afflicted and inspired by his perception that he is the product rather than the producer of several world-shaping discourses. It may be that Grigson's way of talking about poems is not as strictly analytical as this, but the way it teases out the cultural implications and attachments which inhabit any poem's field of force is a critical activity not to be superseded, because it is so closely allied, as an act of reading, to what happens during the poet's act of writing.

A new rhythm, after all, is a new life given to the world, a resuscitation not just of the ear but of the springs of being. The rhythmic disjunctions in Auden's lines, the correspondingly fractured elements of narrative or argument, are wakenings to a new reality, lyric equivalents of the fault he intuited in the life of his times. 'The Watershed' is, according to Edward Mendelson's introduction to *The English Auden*, the earliest of the poems preserved in the standard *Collected Poems*, and reads in places as if a landslide had happened while the lines were being formed or a slippage had occurred between mind and page:

> This land, cut off, will not communicate,
> Be no accessory content to one
> Aimless for faces rather there than here.

What bothered and excluded me when I read this as an undergraduate still excludes me but bothers me no more. The difference is that I am now content that Auden should practise such resistance to the reader's expectations; I take pleasure in its opacity and am ready to accept its obscurity – even if it is wilful – as a symptom of this poet's deliberate insistence upon the distance between art and life. This is not to say that there is no relation between art and life but to insist, as Lazarus in bliss insisted to Dives in torment, that a gulf does exist.

A poem floats adjacent to, parallel to, the historical moment. What happens to us as readers when we board the poem depends upon the kind of relation it displays towards our historical life. Most often, the relation is placatory and palliative, and the poem massages rather than ruffles our sense of what it is to be alive in experience. The usual poem keeps faith with the way we talk at the table, even more with the way we have heard other poems talk to us before. 'Out on the lawn I lie in bed,/ Vega conspicuous overhead/ In the windless nights of June'. Yes, yes, we think; more, more; it's lovely, keep it coming. The melody allays anxiety, the oceanic feeling of womb-oneness stirs, joy fills the spirit's vault like the after-echo of a chorister reverberating in a cathedral:

> That later we, though parted then,
> May still recall these evenings when
> Fear gave his watch no look;
> The lion griefs loped from the shade
> And on our knees their muzzles laid,
> And Death put down his book.

This exemplifies the hymn-singing effect of poetry, its action as a dissolver of differences, and so long as it operates in this mode, poetry functions to produce a sensation of at-homeness and trust in the world. The individual poem may address particular occasions of distress such as a death or a civil war or a recognition of the sad fact of betrayal between lovers, but as long as its tune plays into the prepared expectations of our ear and our nature, as long as desire is not disallowed or allowed only to be disappointed, then the poem's effect will be to offer a sense of possible consolation. It is perhaps because of Auden's susceptibility to this tremblingly delicious power of poetry that he constantly warns against it. 'In so far as poetry, or any other of the arts, can be said to have an ulterior purpose, it is, by telling the truth, to disenchant and disintoxicate.'

Auden, however, practised more enchantment than this pronouncement would suggest, so it is no wonder that he was impelled to keep the critical heckler alive in himself. After the mid-1930s, the iambic melodies and traditional formal obedience of his poems, the skilful rather than sensual deployment of Anglo-Saxon metre in *The Age of Anxiety*, would certainly suggest a weakening of his original refusal of the conventional musics, and a consequent weakening of the newness and otherness of his contribution to the resources, if not to the supply, of poetry itself. As he matured, he may have regretted the scampishness with which he played around in his younger days when, as Christopher Isherwood reports,

> He was very lazy. He hated polishing and making corrections. If I didn't like a poem, he threw it away and wrote another. If I liked one line, he would keep it and work it into a new poem. In this way whole poems were constructed which were simply anthologies of my favourite lines, entirely regardless of grammar or sense. This is the simple explanation of much of Auden's celebrated obscurity.

No doubt, this practice (in so far as Isherwood's blithe account is to be credited) betrays an irresponsibility with regard to comprehensibility but it does represent a strong life-urge in the artist himself. To avoid the consensus and settlement of a meaning which the audience fastens on like a security blanket, to be antic, mettlesome, contrary, to retain the right to impudence, to raise hackles, to harry the audience into wakefulness – to do all this may not only be permissible but necessary if poetry is to keep on coming into a fuller life. Which is why, as I said, I am now ready to attend without anxiety to those oddly unparaphraseable riffs in the very earliest work.

At the beginning of 'The Watershed' the wind is 'chafing', a word which until this occasion had seemed bereft of onomatopoeic life: now it allows us to hear through its lingering vowel and caressing fricative the whisper and friction of wind along a hillside. But this unresisted passage of breath is complicated by the meaning of something rubbing, being fretted and galled and hence inflamed. The word suggests that the topographical crux (of the watershed) which has been left behind is now being experienced as and replaced by a psychological crux, a condition of being subject to two contradictory states, of having to suffer at the same time an utter stillness and a *susurrus* of agitation. Similarly, the grammatical peace of this present participle is disturbed by a lurking middle voice: the grass is chafing, active, but in so far as the only thing being chafed is itself, it is passive. Then, too, the participle occupies a middle state between being transitive and intransitive, and altogether functions like a pass made swiftly, a sleight of semantic hand which unnerves and suspends the reader above a valley of uncertainty. By the second line the reader is already made into that 'stranger' who will be addressed in line nineteen. In fact, the first two words put the reader to the test, for we are not immediately sure whether 'Who stands . . .' initiates a question or a noun clause. This deferral of a sense of syntactical direction is a perfect technical equivalent for that lack of certitude and intuition of imminent catastrophe which gives the poem its soundless climax and closure.

Yet for all the rightness of 'chafing' there is no sense of its having been chosen; it is completely free of that unspoken 'Here be sport for diction-spotters' which hangs over the more deliberate, lexicon-oriented Auden of the last years, when he had begun to resemble in his own person an ample, flopping, ambulatory volume of the OED in carpet slippers. Remember the unravelling wool of the title poem in *Thank You Fog*:

Sworn foe to festination,
daunter of drivers and planes
volants, of course, will curse You,
but how delighted I am
that you've been lured to visit
Wiltshire's witching countryside
for a whole week at Christmas.

That 'witching' is beautiful, permissive, wryly and late-comerly
literary, yet its very relish of its own dexterity is tinged with
tedium, even for the poet (and the same holds, only more so,
for 'festination' and 'volants'). Whereas 'chafing' strikes the
rock of language and brings forth sudden life from the rift,
these later words are collector's items, lifted in huffing pleasure
but without the need and joy which attended the earlier
discovery.

Happily, there is no necessity to go on about this. Later
Auden is a different kind of poetry; by then, the line is
doctrinaire in its domesticity, wanting to comfort like a thread
of wool rather than shock like a bare wire. Attendant upon the
whole performance, there is an unselfpitying air of 'Let us
grieve not, rather find/ Strength in what remains behind', and I
quote the fog passage only to remind you again of the extent to
which Auden's poetry changed its linguistic posture over four
decades. In the very beginning, the stress of Anglo-Saxon
metre and the gnomic clunk of Anglo-Saxon phrasing were
pulled like a harrow against the natural slope of social speech
and iambic lyric. The poem did not sail with the current, it
tangled and hassled, chafed, 'hurt itself on pane, on bark of
elm'. What was happening in such rare musical eddies was
what T. S. Eliot called 'concentration', a term which he
employed when addressing the ever-pressing question of the
relation between emotions actually experienced by the poet and
the emotions which get expressed – or better, get invented – in
a poem. 'We must believe that "emotion recollected in tranquillity" is an inexact formula,' Eliot wrote in 'Tradition and the
Individual Talent', and went on:

For it is neither emotion, nor recollection, nor, without
distortion of meaning, tranquillity. It is a concentration,

and a new thing resulting from the concentration, of a very great number of experiences; it is a concentration which does not happen consciously or of deliberation. These experiences are not 'recollected', and they finally unite in an atmosphere which is 'tranquil' only in that it is a passive attending upon the event.

We are in the presence of such concentration when we read a poem like 'Taller To-day'. This lyric is obviously not meant to fall into step with our usual commonsensical speech-gait, nor is it eager to simulate the emotional and linguistic normality of 'a man speaking to men'; rather it presents us with that 'new thing' which abides, as I suggested, adjacent and parallel to lived experience but which, in spite of perfect sympathy for those living such experience, has no desire to dwell among them:

> Noises at dawn will bring
> Freedom for some, but not this peace
> No bird can contradict: passing, but is sufficient now
> For something fulfilled this hour, loved or endured.

The tranquillity of this has as much to do with what the words achieve as what they recollect. Not, perhaps, the peace which surpasseth understanding, more that which resisteth paraphrasing; a peace, anyhow, 'no bird can contradict'.

But then, after all, does a bird's motion not equal a disturbance or 'contradiction' even within such deep stillness and fulfilment? Yet somehow the bird in the passage hardly attains enough physical presence to be able to contradict anything. For example, if we put it beside Hardy's dew-fall hawk 'crossing the shades to alight/ Upon the wind-warped upland thorn', we know Hardy's to be a dark transience of wing-beat, a palpable, air-lofted glide, a phenomenon *out there*, in the twilight, whereas Auden's bird is an occurrence *in here*, an ignition of energy which happens when certain pert, thin, clicking vowels are combined in a swift reaction: 'but not this peace/ No bird can contradict: passing, but is sufficient now/ For something fulfilled this hour, loved or endured.' The contrapuntal, lengthened-out, interrupted see-saw movement of those lines is as important as their beautifully elaborated and uncomplicating meaning. The hammer of modern English metre, what Robert Graves called the smith-work of *ti-tum, ti-tum*, is going on during the deeper, longer oar-work of Old English, and the ear, no matter how ignorant it may be of the provenance of what it is hearing, attends to the contest. This contest, perfectly matched, undulant yet balanced, is between the navigating efforts of a singular, directed intelligence and the slug and heave of the element in which it toils, the element of language itself.

Auden's work, from beginning to end, is lambent with active intelligence – the greatest intelligence of the twentieth century, in the opinion of Joseph Brodsky. Indeed, Brodsky's essays on Auden, collected in his recent prose volume *Less Than One*, are thrilling evidence of what can happen when 'the words of a dead man are modified in the guts of the living' and a poet finally becomes his admirer. There will be no greater paean to poetry as the breath and finer spirit of all human knowledge than Brodsky's line-by-line commentary on 'September 1, 1939', if commentary is a word applicable to writing so exultant, so grateful and so bracingly *ex cathedra*. He gives definitive credit to Auden's brilliant subjugation of all the traditional poetic means to his own purposes, his melding of rhyme, metre, vocabulary and allusion in the ray of his civilized and ultimately humble mind. Yet it is possible to grant the justice of Brodsky's praise and still regret the passing from Auden's poetry of an element of the uncanny, a trace of the Ralegh *frisson*, of the language's original 'chief woe, world-sorrow'. The price of an art that is so faithfully wedded to disenchantment and disintoxication, that seeks the heraldic shape beneath the rippling skin, that is impelled not only to lay down the law but to keep a civil tongue, the price of all this is a certain diminution of the language's autonomy, a not uncensorious training of its wilder shoots.

Again in Buber's terms, we might say that the more Auden's poetry gained sway over the world of It, the less empowered was its address to the intimate world of Thou. These obscure early poems had been unaccommodating and involuntary efforts to speak the primary and utterly persuasive word. They were, in both the literal and slangier senses of the phrase, 'far out' – even at the times when they kept tight in to the metrical rule and spoke the first language of the child's storybook:

> Starving through the leafless wood
> Trolls run scolding for their food,
> Owl and nightingale are dumb,
> And the angel will not come.
>
> Cold, impossible, ahead
> Lifts the mountain's lovely head
> Whose white waterfall could bless
> Travellers in their last distress.

Although this does not strike back at a rhythmical angle against the expectation of the well-tuned ear, its metaphysical geography remains very different from the consoling contours of the 'real world' of the familiar. Long before the parable poetry of post-war Europe, Auden arrived at a mode that was stricken with premonitions of an awful thing and was adequate to give expression to those premonitions by strictly poetic means. But this unified sensibility fissured when Auden was inevitably driven to extend himself beyond the transmission of intuited knowledge, beyond poetic indirection and implication, and began spelling out those intuitions in a more explicit, analytic and morally ratified rhetoric. In writing a poem like 'Spain', no matter how breathtaking its condensation of vistas or how decent its purpose, or a poem like 'A Summer Night', no matter how Mozartian its verbal equivalent of *agape*, Auden broke with his solitude and his oddity. His responsibility towards the human family became intensely and commendably strong and the magnificently sane, meditative, judicial poems of the 1940s, 1950s and 1960s were the result. We might say that this bonus, which includes such an early masterpiece as 'Letter to Lord Byron' and such a later one as 'In Praise of Limestone', represents an answer to the question posed in 'Orpheus'. That answer inclines to say that 'song' hopes most of all for 'the knowledge of life', and inclines away from the 'bewildered' quotient in the proffered alternative, 'to be bewildered and happy'. To put it another way, Auden finally preferred life to be concentrated into something 'rich' rather than something 'strange', a preference which is understandable if we consider poetry's constant impulse to be all Prospero, harnessed to the rational project of settling mankind into a cosmic security. Yet the doom and omen which characterized the 'strange' poetry of the early 1930s, its bewildered and unsettling visions, brought native English poetry as near as it has ever been to the imaginative verge of the dreadful and offered an example of how insular experience and the universal shock suffered by mankind in the twentieth century could be sounded forth in the English language. In his later poetry, moreover, when a similar note is struck, the poetry inevitably gains in memorability and intensity:

> Unendowed with wealth or pity,
> Little birds with scarlet legs,
> Sitting on their speckled eggs,
> Eye each flu-infected city.
>
> Altogether elsewhere, vast
> Herds of reindeer move across
> Miles and miles of golden moss,
> Silently and very fast.

Lowell's Command

Years ago Michael Longley wrote an essay on poets from Northern Ireland in which he made a distinction between the igneous and the sedimentary as modes of poetic composition. In geology, the igneous rocks were derived from magma or lava solidified below the earth's surface whereas the sedimentary were formed by the deposit and accumulation of mineral and organic materials, worked on, broken down and reconstituted by the action of water, ice and wind. The very sound of the words is suggestive of what is entailed in each case. Igneous is irruptive, unlooked-for and peremptory; sedimentary is steady-keeled, dwelt-upon, graduated.

If, however, the name exists for a process which begins igneous and ends up sedimentary, it would be the one to apply to the poetry of Robert Lowell. Lowell was a poet who had a powerful instinct for broaching the molten stuff early but then he would keep returning to work it over with the hot and cold weathers of his revising intelligence, sometimes even after it had appeared in a book. He was very much alive to the double nature of the act of writing: 'A poem is an event,' he declared to his classes, 'not the record of an event' – equating what I have called *igneous* with *event*, and *sedimentary* with *record*. The distinction comes to light in another form in his *Writers at Work* interview, where he says, 'The revision, the consciousness that tinkers with a poem – that has something to do with teaching and criticism. But the impulse that starts a poem and makes it of any importance is distinct from teaching.' And again, 'I'm sure that writing isn't a craft, that is, something for which you learn the skills and go on turning out. It must come from some deep impulse, deep inspiration.'

Yet the awareness of this distinction between the essential self-engendered impulse and what he would call in the end 'those blessèd structures, plot and rhyme' did not lead Lowell to disdain those structures. His conviction that poetry could not be equated with craft did not diminish his respect for craft. Craft also represents a poet's covenant with his group and his group's language, and that covenant is based on a mutual understanding that the poetic venture is ultimately serviceable no matter how solipsistic it might at first appear. So although when Lowell revised, he was not polishing his lines towards some gleaming neo-classical ideal of 'correctness', he was nevertheless searching for a language that would make the expression of his own self-taste a bolt of clarification not just for himself but for the age. His obsessive subjectivity did not signify an abandonment of the usual life with its attendant moral codes and obligations. On the contrary, Lowell deliberately occupied – sometimes by public apostrophe and rebuke, sometimes by introspective or confessional example – the role of the poet as conscience, one who wakens us to a possible etymology of that word as meaning our capacity to know the same thing together. Such knowing also makes us vulnerable to poetry as a reminder of what, together, we may have chosen to forget, and this admonitory function is one which Robert Lowell exercised, more or less deliberately, all his life.

When I speak of his 'command', however, I am not just thinking of his arrogation of the right to speak to or for an audience, but of the way in which this arrogation is validated by the note of his verse, its particular 'command' over literary tradition and the illiterate ear. Until full middle age, Lowell achieved this authority by tuning his lines in accordance with traditional practice, bringing them to a pitch of tension and intensity by means of musical climax, dramatic gesture or ironical plotting, constantly recalling himself and his reader to an encounter with a formal shape, offering art's frail 'stay against confusion' in the discovery of a firmly verified outline.

It is true that during this first movement of his career, Lowell passed from an ambition to write a stand-offish, self-sufficient poetry to a search for poetry which would achieve a more face-to-face contact with his reader and his reader's world. Yet no matter how close he could or would bring his work to the condition of discourse, he was always seeking to outfox if not to overwhelm the logic of argument by the force of image or oracle. Revelation rather than demonstration was the end he desired. 'The Lord survives the rainbow of his will.' 'Your old-fashioned tirade –/ Loving, rapid, merciless –/ breaks like the Atlantic Ocean on my head.' 'You usually won –/ motionless/ as a lizard in the sun.' Closing lines likes these would tremble in the centre of the ear like an arrow in a target and set the waves of suggestion rippling. A sense of something utterly completed vied with a sense of something startled into scope and freedom. The reader was permitted the sensation of a whole meaning simultaneously clicking shut and breaking open, a momentary illusion that the fulfilments which were being experienced in the ear spelled out meanings and fulfilments available in the world. So, no matter how much the poem insisted on break-down or the evacuation of meaning from experience, its fall toward a valueless limbo was broken by the perfectly stretched safety net of poetic form itself.

Life Studies, for example, noted at first for the extremity of its candour, so apparently private and self-absorbed, now stands as firm and approachable as a public monument. It silhouettes its figures against the life of the times; its hard, intelligent lines and the tone of comprehension informing its well-braced speech imply that there is a social dimension to what it is voicing. It trusts that it has an audience and hence it is able to proceed to the outrageous or unnerving business of auto-biography with a certain air of courtesy. Lowell may write:

> Terrible that old life of decency
> without unseemly intimacy
> or quarrels, when the unemancipated woman
> still had her Freudian papà and maids!

Yet the decorum of *Life Studies* is continuous with that old life even as it reveals its disintegration, its inadequate hauteur in the face of locked razors, mad soldiers and electric chairs. This decorum, the book's technical mastery and its drive towards impersonality, are as much part of Lowell's birthright as his patronymic. As an artist, he was the proper Bostonian with his back to a wall of tradition. His poetic art, however self-willed it might on occasion be, could never escape from an innate demand that it should not just be a self-indulgence. There had to be something surgical in the incisions he made, something professional and public-spirited in the exposure. The whole thing was a test, of himself and of the resources of poetry, and in *Life Studies* those resources proved themselves capable of taking new strains, in both the musical and stressful sense of that word.

Lowell did not innocently lisp in numbers. Innocence was not something he set much store by anyhow, either in himself or in others, and his whole *œuvre* is remarkably free of the sigh for lost Eden. Everything begins outside the garden, in the learning process, in sweat and application. No lisps. The voice has broken by the time it speaks. It has been to school, literally as well as figuratively. Lowell's first style, it should not be forgotten, was formed in the English Departments of Kenyon College, Vanderbilt College and Louisiana State University. His mentors, true enough, were poets and knew poetry inside out, yet they were equally and more famously teachers of poetry, New Critics driven by a passion to pluck out the last secret of any poem by unearthing, if necessary, its seventh ambiguity. No wonder then that Lowell, in a late poem, wryly and accurately likened his early work to the seven-walled fortress of Troy, where meaning lay immured behind rings of highly intended art. But at least that meant that he wrote, in the words of F. W. Dupee, 'as if poetry were still a major art and not merely a venerable pastime'. Among a strenuous and brilliant generation of poet-critics, praying to be obsessed by writing and having their prayers answered, Lowell strove to hold his own not only by mastering the classical, English, European and American poetic canons; he also strove to outstrip the level best of his peers by swerves that were all his own: doctrinal, ancestral, political. Doctrinal, when he converted to the Roman Catholic Church and betrayed not just a faith but a civic solidarity. Ancestral, when he invoked his dynastic right derived from the Winslows and the Lowells and presumed to speak like a curator of American history and culture. Political, when he went to jail as a conscientious objector in 1943, having nevertheless volunteered (without response) for the Navy and the Army in the previous year.

It was in this act of conscientious objection that doctrine, ancestry and politics fused themselves in one commanding stroke and Lowell succeeded in uniting the aesthetic instinct with the obligation to witness morally and significantly in the realm of public action. Moreover, with what William Meredith once called his 'crooked brilliance', Lowell had combined public dissent with psychic liberation; the refusal of the draft was an affront to the family, another strike in the war of individuation and disengagement which he had so forcefully initiated when he flattened his father with one rebellious blow during his first year at Harvard in the late 1930s. Altogether, the refusal to enlist burst up from some deep magma and had a sort of igneous personal scald to it. It may have been the manic statement of a 'fire-breathing CO' but it did burn with a powerful disdainful rhetoric of election and recrimination.

President Roosevelt was first of all morally wrong-footed in Lowell's covering letter – 'You will understand how painful such a decision is for an American whose family traditions, like your own, have always found their fulfillment in maintaining . . . our country's freedom and honor.' Then, in the public statement called 'Declaration of Personal Responsibility', the whole of American democracy was arraigned for its Machiavellian contempt for the laws of justice and charity between nations. In its determination to wage a war 'without quarter or principles, to the permanent destruction of Germany and Japan', the United States was allying itself with 'the demagoguery and herd hypnosis of the totalitarian tyrannies' and had criminalized the good patriotic war begun in response to aggression in 1941. The usual summaries of this document tend to focus on Lowell's outrage at the Allies' immense indifference to the lives of civilians when they bombed Hamburg and the Ruhr; the main drift, as I understand it, is to accuse the United States of becoming like the tyrannies which it set out to oppose. Therefore, the statement concludes:

after long deliberation on my responsibilities to myself, my country, and my ancestors who played responsible parts in its making, I have come to the conclusion that I cannot honorably participate in a war whose prosecution, as far as I can judge, constitutes a betrayal of my country.

Not unexpectedly, one detects here something of the note of a speech from the dock. Yet even granting that the profile is carefully posed for chivalric effect and that there is a certain strut to the moral carriage of the rhetoric, Lowell does achieve a credible and dignified withdrawal of assent from the deplorable direction affairs were beginning to take. In fact, and in spite of the enormous difference between the gravity of the occasions, this is not unlike Yeats, on the first night of Sean O'Casey's *The Plough and the Stars*, rebuking the audience of the Abbey Theatre for disgracing themselves 'again' – which meant, of course, that they had thereby disgraced *him*. In each case, the habit of command was something which issued from the poet's caste. Admittedly, neither Yeats nor Lowell came from a family immediately involved in government or public affairs, but they did nevertheless inhale a sense of responsibility for their country, their culture and the future of both.

It was, however, characteristic of Lowell to have manoeuvred himself into a position where he could speak with superior force. It was rarely, with him, a case of 'Let this cup pass', but rather a matter of 'How can I get my hands *on* the cup'. Between the stylistic ardour of his early poems and such thoroughly plotted and savoured moments as the draft refusal, there is a discernible connection. It has to do with the determination to force an issue by pressure of will, by the plotting instinct which he would ultimately castigate in himself because as a result of it he had ended up 'not avoiding injury to others' or to himself; it had to do, in other words, with the tactical, critical revising side of his nature. Lowell was always one to call out the opposition, to send the duelling note; so there was an imperious strain even in his desire to embrace the role of witness. Yet the desire was authentic and can bear comparison with a corresponding moment of collision between individual moral conscience and the demands of the historical moment in the life of Osip Mandelstam.

Mandelstam, of course, lived in a tyranny and Lowell lived in a democracy. That is literally a vital distinction. Nevertheless, I do not think it improper to set the crisis faced by Lowell in 1943 beside the crisis faced by the Russian poet in the early 1930s. At that time, after five years of poetic silence during which he had tried to make some inner accommodation with a Soviet reality which his nature instinctively rejected, Mandelstam had done something quite uncharacteristic. He wrote his one and only poem of direct political comment, a set of couplets contemptuous of Stalin; and he compounded the crime by composing another document of immense rage and therapeutic force called 'Fourth Prose'. Both were self-cleansing acts and tragic preparations. Even though they dared not present themselves as public statements like Lowell's 'Declaration of Personal Responsibility', they were ultimate declarations of that very responsibility and would lead not to prison but to death. It was as if Mandelstam were cutting the hair off his own neck in a gesture that signified his readiness for the guillotine; yet this was the only way in which his true voice and being could utter themselves, the only way in which his self-justification could occur. After this moment, the hedonism and jubilation of purely lyric creation developed an intrinsically moral dimension. The poet's double responsibility to tell a truth as well as to make a thing would henceforth be singly discharged in the formal achievement of the individual poem.

It would be an exaggeration and an insolence to equate Lowell's gesture with Mandelstam's sacrifice; yet I would suggest that Lowell's justification of his specifically poetry-writing self was bound up with his protest and his experience of jail – in the same way as Mandelstam's airy liberation was earned at an even more awful price. Jail set the *maudit* sign upon the brow of the blue-blooded boy. It made him the republic's Villon rather than its Virgil. It permitted him to feel that the discharge of violent energy from the cauldron of his nature had a positive witnessing function, that by forging a poetic sound which echoed the resolute hammering within his nature, he was forging a conscience for the times.

So the robust Symbolist opacity of the first books probably derives at least in part from some such personally authenticated conviction about the autonomous force of poetry. West Street

Jail and the Danbury Correction Center provided a spiritual licence to withdraw from the language of the compromised tribe and reinforced that old habit of making the poetic task a matter of dense engagement with the purely literary resources of the medium itself. The percussion and brass section of the language orchestra is driven hard and, in a great early set-piece like 'The Quaker Graveyard in Nantucket', the string section hardly gets a look-in. Distraught woodwinds surge across the soundscape; untamed and inconsolable discords ride the blast. Hart Crane, Dylan Thomas, Arthur Rimbaud, Lycidas himself – resurrected as a language of turbulent sea-sound – all of them press in at the four corners of the page, taut-cheeked genii of storm, intent on blowing their power into the blank centre of an Eastern Seaboard chart. The reader is caught in a gale-force of expressionism and could be forgiven for thinking that Aeolus has it in for him personally. Here is, for example, Section III of the poem:

> When the whale's viscera go and the roll
> Of its corruption shall overrun this world,
> Beyond tree-swept Nantucket and Woods Hole
> And Martha's Vineyard, Sailor, will your sword
> Whistle and fall and sink into the fat?
> In the great ash-pit of Jehoshaphat
> The bones cry for the blood of the white whale,
> The fat flukes arch and whack about its ears,
> The death-lance churns into the sanctuary, tears
> The gun-blue swingle, heaving like a flail,
> And hacks the coiling life out: it works and drags
> And rips the sperm-whale's midriff into rags,
> Gobbets of blubber spill to wind and weather,
> Sailor, and gulls go round the stoven timbers
> Where the morning stars sing out together
> And thunder shakes the white surf and dismembers
> The red flag hammered in the mast-head. Hide,
> Our steel, Jonas Messias, in Thy side.

It is thrilling to put out in these poetic conditions, to feel what Yeats called 'the stirring of the beast', to come into the presence of sovereign diction and experience the tread of something metrical, conscious and implacable. To say that such poetry has designs upon us is about as understated as to say that Zeus introduced himself to Leda in fancy dress. 'Take note, Hopkins,' it cries. 'Take note, Melville. And reader, take that!' Yet to enter a poetic career at this pitch was to emulate Sam Goldwyn's quest for the ultimate in movie excitement – something beginning with an earthquake and working up to a climax. It was to create a monotone of majesty which was bound to drown out the human note of the poet who had aspired to majesty in the first place. Lawrence had talked about the young poet putting his hand over his daimon's mouth but Lowell actually handed it a megaphone. Somehow the thing would have to be toned down or else the command established would quickly devolve into cacophony, into something unmodulated and monomaniacal.

During the next decade, while a new style was being meditated, the shape of Lowell's life was also being established. Maybe in spite of the cruel cycles of mania and industry, maybe because of them, Lowell wrote extraordinarily and achieved eminence. By the time of his marriage to Elizabeth Hardwick and his entry upon the New York scene, he was a consolidated literary phenomenon, with the Pulitzer Prize and the Poetry Consultancy at the Library of Congress already behind him. One cannot ever be sure to what extent the crenellated mass of the early verse was a fortification against the illness of his mind, or an emanation of it, but there is no doubting the definitive strength of the work itself. What I want to focus upon now, however, is the not uncommon spectacle of a poet with just such a dear-won individual style facing into his forties and knowing that it will all have to be done again. Words by Anna Swir, whom I quoted in the first of these lectures, are again apposite:

> The goal of words in poetry is to grow up to the contents, yet that goal cannot ever be attained, for only a small part of the psychic energy which dwells in a poet incarnates itself in words. In fact, every poem has the right to ask for a new poetics . . . We could say in a paradoxical abbrevia-

tion that a writer has two tasks. The first – to create one's own style. The second – to destroy one's own style. The second is more difficult and takes more time.

Lowell did this second thing twice in his poetic life, and on each occasion knew what he was doing – which made it both more purposeful and more painstaking. When I say that he knew what he was doing, I do not mean that he had a prearranged programme of what he wished to achieve, some poetic equivalent of the blueprint in a painting-by-numbers kit. It is rather that he was so intently literary and the critical, teaching side of his mind was so unremittingly active that his command as a poet was never without self-consciousness, without – in the good Elizabethan sense – cunning. He had been imprinted with the idea of 'poetic development' by the immediate examples of the careers of Yeats, Eliot and Auden and by the insistent pressure of minds like Randall Jarrell's and Allen Tate's; yet only a sensibility with a core of volcanic individual genius could have survived a professional buffing like the one which Lowell's had undergone from these and other quarters. He could easily have got himself jammed in a Parnassian impasse; instead, the epoch-making *Life Studies* appeared in 1959, when Lowell was forty-two. Anna Swir's law was being proved for the first time in his career. He was later to recollect this period of his life in a well-known account of his experience of reading his symbol-ridden and wilfully difficult early poems in California, to audiences accustomed to the loose-weave writing of the Beats. Already he had sensed 'that most of what he knew about writing was a hindrance', that his old work was 'stiff, humorless and encumbered by its ponderous stylistic armor'.

I am not, however, going to rehearse further the attributes of the masterful new poetry which broke from the tegument of his old rhetoric. The main point to insist on is its freedom from the anxiety to sound canonical, the way it has discovered a site for its authority not by the assimilation of literary tradition but upon the basis of the roused poetic voice. A phrase of Mandelstam's will once again do critical service here, one which comes from his prose work, *Journey to Armenia*. In writing this prose, Mandelstam was blinded with the knowledge he had been trying to suppress, namely that his poetry arose out of an unregenerate, pre-revolutionary sensibility which was responsible not to imposed constraints but to natural processes, those simultaneously proffered by the phenomena of the world and engendered by the frolic of language. His expression of this renewed awareness was intense and oblique, as when he exclaimed: 'If I believe in the shadow of the oak and the steadfastness of speech articulation, how can I appreciate the present age?'

'The steadfastness of speech articulation': it is a phrase which characterizes the dominant music of Lowell's poetic prime, from *Life Studies* through *For the Union Dead* and *Near the Ocean*. But it also directs us to the very source of that music, in conviction of the tongue's right to speak freely and soundingly, and a further conviction of its capacity, if not to unveil reality, then significantly to enrich it. For while these books often tangle with a great heavy web of subject-matter, autobiographical, cultural and political, they are not primarily interested in commentary or opinion about such subject-matter. Nor are they primarily interested in building stanzas like warehouses to store it. Rather they are interested in how to make an event of it, how to project forms and energies in terms of it. They are not, of course, successful all the time, but when they do succeed, they rest their claims upon no authority other than the jurisdiction and vigour of their own artistic means.

The patrician repose of 'middle Lowell', the distance travelled from the anxious majesty of the early style, shows up significantly when we compare the protest Lowell made against his society's waging of war in the 1940s with the one he made against the Vietnam War in the 1960s. On this later occasion, his refusal of an invitation to President Johnson's White House was done without much clamour or histrionics. It was no longer a case of the writer putting himself to the test by taking on the role of bard and scapegoat. It was now rather the President who was to be on the defensive. Poetry, in the figure of this silvered Brahmin from Boston, was calling upon policy to account for itself. Yet Lowell's authority now resided in the mystery of his achieved art rather than in his ancestry or in the justice of any public controversy he might choose to initiate:

When I was telephoned last week and asked to read at the White House Festival of the Arts on June fourteenth, I am afraid I accepted somewhat rapidly and greedily. I thought of such an occasion as a purely artistic flourish, even though every serious artist knows that he cannot enjoy public celebration without making subtle public commitments. After a week's wondering, I have decided that I am conscience-bound to refuse your courteous invitation.

The books of Lowell's middle years, like this grave and well-judged political protest, are wise to the world and wise about it. 'For the Union Dead' and 'Waking Early Sunday Morning' are two of the finest public poems of our time but they do not address the world in order to correct it. They Lowellize it instead, make it ring, make it a surface against which the poet's voice strikes, is caught and thereby either amplifies itself or glances off. Here it is, amplifying, at the conclusion of 'Waking Early':

> Pity the planet, all joy gone
> from this sweet volcanic cone;
> peace to our children when they fall
> in small war on the heels of small
> war – until the end of time
> to police the earth, a ghost
> orbiting forever lost
> in our monotonous sublime.

And here it is, in 'Middle Age', glancing off:

> Father, forgive me
> my injuries,
> as I forgive
> those I
> have injured!
>
> You never climbed
> Mount Sion, yet left
> dinosaur

[*140*]

death-steps on the crust,
where I must walk.

There will be more to say about this less assertive voice before
we finish, but for the moment let us salute it as a good victory
by Lowell over his ruling passion for sounding victorious, his
temptation to raise the trumpet or let the left hand reinforce the
right with a strongly affirmative or discordant bass. As he
himself well knew, there was 'an incomparable wandering
voice' within him which he often and habitually made the
captive of what he also called his 'maze of iron composition'.

Those phrases come from the lovely, limber final sonnet of
Lowell's book *The Dolphin* and thus form the last lines of the
massive triptych composed in his fifties, comprising ultimately
the three books called *History*, *For Lizzie and Harriet*, and *The
Dolphin*. If I here skim over the mighty heave of this work, it is
not because I miss Lowell's command in the sound of its lines.
On the contrary. These astonishingly, wilfully strong lines are
too much under the sway of an imposed power. There is no
doubt about the good artistic intentions of what he is doing,
and no doubt about the foundry heat in which scores of the
standard-mould, fourteen-line, unrhymed poem-ingots are
being smelted and cast. To change the metaphor, one admires
once again the spectacle of a poet taking the crowbar to a
perfected style: these new, unmelodious, impacted forms are
deliberate rebukes to the classical cadences of the volumes of
the 1960s. Line by line, in local manifestations, the genius and
sinuousness are still alive and well, but to confront the whole
triptych is to confront a phalanx. I feel driven off the field of my
reader's freedom by the massive riveted façade, the armoured
tread, the unconceding density of it all.

What I wish to dwell upon instead is the gentler, autumnal
work in Lowell's last collection, *Day by Day*. The effect of
coming to it after the twelve-tone scale of these previous books
is of moving from a works-floor ringing with the occasional
treble beauty of that busy crowbar to a room full of canvases by,
say, Bonnard. A roseate benevolence in the pigment, an
unextinguished but ungreedy sensuality in the air, a warm-
bloodedness at the centre or in the offing. The voice comes from

pillow level rather than from a podium, indulgent but unfooled, schooled by mutuality but not yet schooled into mutuality, more inclined to wryness than pathos. It can cover a great distance in a single shift of tone or image or line. The typical effects are of ruminant talk ('Marriage' and 'Last Walk') or skewed proverbial wisdom ('For Sheridan') or a cross-cutting of these styles into each other ('Ants'). All of this does come, as a character in one of the poems desires it to, 'a little nearer/ the language of the tribe', but its primary purpose is neither to curry favour with the reader nor to keep in ideological step with writing in the American grain. The poems proceed by free association, as Helen Vendler has observed; they are as tousled, amiably importunate and comfortably unpredictable as lovers weaving through warm rooms at the end of a slightly erotic, slightly drunken party.

All the same, the tone is not familiar or insinuatingly personal. There is a curious sensation of being kept at a remove while still being close enough to feel the excitement of impulses translating themselves into phrases. The mode pretends to dramatic personal utterance – Lowell talking to his wife, best friends, his son, himself – yet it keeps breaking into a note which is random, impersonal and oracular; 'things thrown in air', as one poem says, 'alive in flight', things resembling the scrapings that fly when 'the immortal is scraped unconsenting from the mortal'.

Lowell always had an inclination to launch such single lines and phrases across the sky of the poem and indeed, in the blank sonnets had so tried to make poems blaze line by line that the reader could feel at times he was out bareheaded in a meteor shower. Those poems were not so much loaded with ore as packed with gold fillings, biting in order to gleam. In *Day by Day*, however, his ferocity of intent has been calmed and replaced by a temperate waft of either image or generalization. 'The elder flower is champagne', says one line which sails above the discourse of 'Milgate'. 'A false calm is the best calm', says an orphaned line in 'Suburban Surf'. And so on: 'If you keep cutting your losses,/ you have no loss to cut' ('In the Ward'). 'If they have you by the neck, a rope will be found' ('Domesday Book').

We have come far indeed from the kind of command this poet sought and exercised in the early work, where truth was piledriven by metre and condensed allusions. Now the command is achieved by the oddly tilted wisdom of the propositions, their oblique clarity and applicability, their wistful strangeness. The tone is not forced or forcing, the voice of the poem does not come down upon you but rises towards its own surface. There is an aqueous rather than an igneous quality now to the poem's beginnings and emergence, nowhere more than in the opening poem of the volume called 'Ulysses and Circe', especially in Section V. This is my favourite moment in the book. In the opening lines, Lowell retains an old bravura and at the end touches a muted Homeric note of landfall. What happens in between is kaleidoscopic, a progress of gnomic stanzas, little poem fragments in themselves, held together by the memory and voice of Ulysses.

This Ulysses comes on as a man on the verge of being posthumous to himself, ventriloquizing (through the autobiographical voice of Robert Lowell) about his interlude with Circe, his sensual self-knowledge and his appeased curiosities. Ulysses begins the poem as a drowsy voluptuary and will end it as a killer about to strike, thus acting as a kind of correlative for the poet caught between his marriages and his manias. The poem is spoken in a middle voice, neither dramatic monologue exactly nor confessional lyric: enclosed in quotation marks, it rides an eddying course between the near shore of autobiography and the farther shore of myth:

> 'Long awash and often touching bottom
> by the sea's great green go-light
> I found my exhaustion
> the light of the world.
>
> Earth isn't earth
> if my eyes are on the moon,
> her likeness caught
> in the split second of vacancy –
>
> duplicitous,
> open to all men, unfaithful.

After so many millennia,
Circe,
are you tired
of turning swine to swine?

How can I please you,
if I am not a man?

I have grown bleak-boned with survival –
I who hoped to leave the earth
younger than I came.

Age is the bilge
we cannot shake from the mop.

Age walks on our faces –
at the tunnel's end,
if faith can be believed,
our flesh will grow lighter.'

This poem does have its openness, yet at its core there is an intransigently charmless streak, and it is the combination of neuter stillness at the centre with something more tolerant and glamorous on the surface which makes it continuous with one of the loveliest and strangest moments in Lowell's early work. I am thinking of the Walsingham section of 'The Quaker Graveyard at Nantucket', where the locus of stillness was in the face of the statue of the Virgin which, 'expressionless, expresses God'. Around this pivotal omphalos of the unlovely, the oceanic symphonies swayed and thundered, and they depended upon the statue's quietude more than upon the massed instruments of the vocabulary for their ultimate effects of turbulence and tragedy. The face was like a star whose light was forever at the moment of arrival, an energy source. Why this figure of the Virgin should enter the poem could be explained intellectually by contrasting her with the predatory, Calvinist, blood-spilling whalers; poetically speaking, however, we sense its rightness as a matter of emotional effect, a result of its timing and placing. What it supplies is what T. S. Eliot was wanting to supply in 'Little Gidding' when he wrote to John Hayward:

> The defect of the whole poem, I feel, is the lack of some
> acute personal reminiscence (never to be explicated, of
> course, but to give power from well below the surface).

It is just this sensation of power coming from below the surface,
without any need for its explication, which the reader finds in
the Walsingham section of 'The Quaker Graveyard'.

I have digressed because I want to suggest that the virtue of
the best poems in *Day by Day* derives from their being similarly
sustained by the up-draft of energy from 'acute personal
reminiscence'. Yet the reminiscence is itself unmysterious,
coming from a recent past or a just-sped present: what is
uncanny is the feeling of being at the eye of an agitation, in an
emotional calm that is completely impersonal, a condition
evenly distanced from the infinite indifference on the minus
side of the graph and the infinite serenity at the other extreme.
At his best, Lowell can find the co-ordinates for this point and
beam in on a state that is neither stasis nor crisis, more dynamic
than the former, less precarious than the latter. At less inspired
moments, this genuine impassiveness is simulated: we
encounter in its place an unremitting verbal determination to
secure our dazed attention – something which happens often
enough in the books of blank sonnets to make the experience of
reading them disorienting.

Nothing disorienting about the poetry we have just read,
however, *qua* poetry, no matter how disconcerting the things it
has to say about ageing and ending: 'Age is the bilge/ we cannot
shake from the mop.' Repudiation, ripeness, greyness, aggra-
vation – it's all there, in the very mouthing of the syllables, from
the not unpalatable fruity corruption of 'age is the bilge', with
its custardy vowels and gelatinate consonants, to the shudder
and ineffectual vigour of 'we cannot shake from the mop'. This
is heady and disintoxicating all at once, exactly the kind of
wisdom to vindicate the claim to preternatural clarity and
utmost endurance earlier on: 'I found my exhaustion/ the light
of the world.' This poem manages to begin and to carry on from
the point where *Samson Agonistes* ended in 'calm of mind, all
passion spent'. It is the poetic anti-world to the world of Sam
Goldwyn's apocalyptic beginnings. Unlike the post-modern

voice which speaks in Derek Mahon's 'Lives' and 'knows too much to know anything any more', Lowell's speaker retains a kind of ultimate heuristic joy. Even though the single-minded-ness of Dante's Ulysses would seem to him simple-minded, and the rhetoric of Tennyson's incredible, the omniscient tone of this veteran sexual campaigner does not preclude the possibility of further excitements. If the cadences do not move with any great long-swelled promise, neither have they cancelled all expectation of a renewed shock from experience.

It all represents a final commanding emergence of the style which once sweetened sour subjects a decade and a half earlier in *For the Union Dead*. There, in the first poems of acute personal reminiscence, 'Water' and 'The Old Flame', and in that seemingly casual gloss called 'Middle Age', Lowell relaxed the method of decisive confrontation which he had pursued in *Life Studies*. Now, the battened ferocity of intelligence which characterized the earlier work was replaced by a mood still vigilant and nervy, but not as feral or intensely directed.

This 'relaxed' poetry in *For the Union Dead* prefigures the achievement of the best work in *Day by Day*. It wakens rather than fixes. A few strokes, a notation, a bestirring and a saluting, such casual means are typical of writing which is not in itself just casual notation: little riddling units are lifted up into the condition of poetry. These poems are pre-eminently events rather than the record of events – as that wonderfully chaste and bare-handed poem 'Fall 1961' demonstrates:

> All autumn, the chafe and jar
> of nuclear war;
> we have talked our extinction to death.
> I swim like a minnow
> behind my studio window.
>
> Our end drifts nearer,
> the moon lifts,
> radiant with terror.
> The state
> is a diver under a glass bell.
>
> A father's no shield
> for his child.

> We are like a lot of wild
> spiders crying together,
> but without tears.

At such a moment, Lowell's poetry is beautifully equal to its occasion. It does not flex its literary muscle. Its tone is unemphatic yet it derives from a kind of wisdom which knows itself to be indispensable even as it takes itself for granted. I suggest that Lowell's command finally came to reside in this self-denial, this readiness not to commandeer the poetic event but to let his insights speak their own riddling truths:

> Past fifty, we learn with surprise and a sense
> of suicidal absolution
> that what we intended and failed
> could never have happened –
> and must be done better.

The Indefatigable Hoof-taps: Sylvia Plath

I have mentioned before the poet's need to get beyond ego in order to become the voice of more than autobiography. At the level of poetic speech, when this happens, sound and meaning rise like a tide out of language to carry individual utterance away upon a current stronger and deeper than the individual could have anticipated.

Different poets have had different ideas about how this is achieved. For Robert Frost, there was an original cadencing which he called 'the sound of sense' and which he considered the precondition of poetry: the melodies of individual poems had to re-enact this sound before they could be heard as given and inevitable. It is as if the poem is a single walker, stepping into the procession of language, falling naturally into step with its common pace and massed, unforced footfall. When Frost spoke of 'sentence sounds' and 'tones' as vocal entities in themselves, predestined contours of the voice, previous to content and articulated meaning, he was clearly anxious to affirm poetry's indigenous rights by establishing its conformity to these linguistic norms.

T. S. Eliot was also much exercised by the idea that poetry housed older and deeper levels of energy than those supplied by explicit meaning and immediate rhythmic stimulus. This is his formulation of 'the auditory imagination': it is

the feeling for syllable and rhythm, penetrating far below the conscious levels of thought and feeling, invigorating every word; sinking to the most primitive and forgotten, returning to an origin and bringing something back . . . fusing the most ancient and most civilized mentalities.

Once again, as in the case of Frost, there is a defensive and self-justifying motive at work in all this. What is implicit here is an argument for the deep humanity of the achieved poem, its access to an evolutionary racial ear. The auditory imagination not only unites for the poet the most ancient and most civilized mentalities; it also unites reader and poet and poem in an experience of enlargement, of getting beyond the confines of the first person singular, of widening the lens of receptivity until it reaches and is reached by the world beyond the self.

Yeats also speaks of writing for the ear, like the old writers of the world, but he is less concerned in his criticism to speak about the actual tones and strains of poetic language than to evoke the impersonal, impersonating, mask-like utterance which he takes all poetry to be. We are reminded how *persona* derives from *personare*, meaning 'to sound out through', how the animation of verb lives in the mask's noun-like impassiveness. For Yeats, the poet is somebody who is spoken through. He is reborn in his art as something intended and complete. The firmness of an achieved style represents a victory over subjectivity and a capacity for being possessed by archetypal voice. Poetry, drama and myth converge, what all humankind has known and experienced is potentially available through the ceremony of the poem and thus, once again, the poem's right to its place in the world, its universal validity, is secured.

I remind you of these different apologies, verifications and explanations of poetry, vocal, aural and dramatic/mythic, because they are all germane to a consideration of the achievement of Sylvia Plath, a poet who grew to a point where she permitted herself identification with the oracle and gave herself over as a vehicle for possession; a poet who sought and found a style of immediate speech, animated by the tones of a voice speaking excitedly and spontaneously; a poet governed by the auditory imagination to the point where her valediction to life consisted of a divesting of herself into words and echoes. 'Words', one of the last half-dozen poems she wrote in February 1963, is the source of the title of this lecture:

> Axes
> After whose stroke the wood rings,

And the echoes!
Echoes travelling
Off from the centre like horses.

The sap
Wells like tears, like the
Water striving
To re-establish its mirror
Over the rock

That drops and turns,
A white skull,
Eaten by weedy greens.
Years later I
Encounter them on the road –

Words dry and riderless,
The indefatigable hoof-taps.
While
From the bottom of the pool, fixed stars
Govern a life.

I shall be referring to this poem later, but for the moment I want
it to stand as a reminder of the kind of poetry which Sylvia Plath
achieved in her volume *Ariel* and in the poems which preceded
it. This was the poetry in which, as Judith Kroll has suggested,
she allowed her autobiographical self to identify with her mask
as inspired poet, and it possesses a freedom and peremptori-
ness which is altogether distinctive. It represents the final stage
of her artistic achievement, which obviously and notoriously
was linked to developments in her psychological and domestic
life. To put it briefly, in Yeats's terms: from October 1962 until
her death in 1963, Sylvia Plath did not live as a bundle of
accident and incoherence; she did not sit down to breakfast but
sat down to write; she woke already composed into 'something
intended, complete', feeling 'like a very efficient tool or weapon
used and in demand from moment to moment'. On 29 September, just before the deluge of new work began, she writes to
Aurelia Plath:

Dearest Mother, It is going on 6.30 in the morning, and I
am a woman in my study, Pifco going, with my first cup of
morning coffee.

On 12 October, the breakthrough is complete:

Every morning, when my sleeping pill wears off, I am up
about five, in my study with coffee, writing like mad –
have managed a poem a day before breakfast. All book
poems. Terrific stuff, as if domesticity had choked me.

It was in this mood that she wrote the work in which Robert
Lowell remarked 'perfect control, like the control of a skier who
avoids every death-trap until reaching the final drop' –
although it should be said that Lowell's image of the death-trap
is derived from hindsight as much as from the poems themselves.

The great appeal of *Ariel* and its constellated lyrics is the
feeling of irresistible given-ness. There inheres in this poetry a
sense of surprised arrival, of astonished being. The poems were
written quickly and they transmit to the reader something of
the unexpectedness of their own becoming. There is the
pressure of absolute *fiat* behind them: a set of images springs
into presence and into motion as at a whimsical but unignorable
command. They represent the extreme extension of the imagist
mode, which Pound characterized as expressing an emotional
and intellectual complex in a moment of time. Their metamorphic speed and metaphoric eagerness are boosted by the logic
of their own associative power, and they rush towards whatever conclusions are inherent in their elements. These poems
are the vehicles of their own impulses, and it was entirely right
that the title which gathered them together should not only
recall Shakespeare's pure spirit but also the headlong gallop of a
runaway horse. They are full of exhilaration in themselves, the
exhilaration of a mind that creates in some sort of mocking
spirit, outstripping the person who has suffered. They move
without hesitation and assume the right to be heard; they, the
poems, are what we attend to, not the poet. They are, in
Lowell's words, events rather than the records of events, and as
such represent the triumph of Sylvia Plath's romantic ambition

to bring expressive power and fully achieved selfhood into congruence. The tongue proceeds headily into its role as governor; it has located the source where the fixed stars are reflected and from which they transmit their spontaneous and weirdly trustworthy signals.

But before all this could occur, Plath's tongue was itself governed by the disciplines of metre, rhyme, etymology, assonance, enjambment. Even if her husband had not given us an image of her as the obedient neophyte, we could have deduced it from the procedures of her early verse. 'She wrote her early poems very slowly,' Ted Hughes tells us, 'thesaurus open on her knee, in her large, strange handwriting, like a mosaic, where every letter stands separate within the work, a hieroglyph to itself . . . Every poem grew complete from its own root, in that laborious inching way, as if she were working out a mathematical problem, chewing her lips, putting a thick dark ring of ink around each word that stirred her on the page of the thesaurus.' That would have been in the late 1950s, when Sylvia Plath was preparing the volume which would be published in 1960 in England as *The Colossus*, in the course of which she gradually focused her poetic attention inward and found a characteristic method of self-exploration.

This was sometimes based on the allegorization of personal experience into an emblem or icon, sometimes on the confounding of the autobiographical and the mythological. 'Full Fathom Five' and 'Lorelei', two poems based on her reading of Jacques Cousteau, are typical examples of this latter procedure. The autobiographical matter they draw upon includes the death of her father when she was a child of eight and the family's subsequent move inland from the sea, after which, as Plath wrote in 'Ocean 1212-W', 'those first nine years of my life sealed themselves off like a ship in a bottle – beautiful, inaccessible, obsolete, a fine, white flying myth.' The autobiographical element also includes a recognition of her suicide attempt in August 1953, and obviously takes some cognizance of the psychiatric treatment which ensued, with its conscious attempts at self-comprehension and self-renewal. But all this is secluded behind the literary and mythological aspects of the poems themselves, which are the products of a ripening skill.

What I propose, therefore, is to examine a number of characteristic poems from different periods of Plath's astonishingly swift development, in order to rehearse again the kind of poetic phenomenon which she represents, and in order to witness the spectacle of a gifted writer becoming a definitive one. I want to consider all this as a literary venture with a manifestly salutary purpose in the poet's life, but I shall also have to say something about how the purely artistic force of her achievement became involved with other strains in the culture she inhabited, and how an action which was essentially triumphant came to be read as punitive.

I find in her poetic journey three stages which seem to exemplify three degrees of poetic achievement, and since I have always found it instructive to read a famous passage of Wordsworth as a parable of these three stages, I shall do so here in particular relation to Sylvia Plath's career. The passage in question is the one where Wordsworth writes about his young self whistling through his fingers to arouse the owls so that they would then call back to him; but it especially evokes certain moments when he would be imposed upon by the power of the whole natural universe:

There was a Boy; ye knew him well, ye cliffs
And islands of Winander! – many a time,
At evening, when the earliest stars began
To move along the edges of the hills,
Rising or setting, would he stand alone
Beneath the trees, or by the glimmering lake;
And there, with fingers interwoven, both hands
Pressed closely palm to palm and to his mouth
Uplifted, he, as through an instrument,
Blew mimic hootings to the silent owls,
That they might answer him. – And they would shout
Across the watery vale, and shout again,
Responsive to his call, – with quivering peals,
And long halloos, and screams, and echoes loud
Redoubled and redoubled; concourse wild
Of jocund din! And, when there came a pause
Of silence such as baffled his best skill:

[153]

Then, sometimes, in that silence, while he hung
Listening, a gentle shock of mild surprise
Has carried far into his heart the voice
Of mountain-torrents; or the visible scene
Would enter unawares into his mind
With all its solemn imagery, its rocks,
Its woods, and that uncertain heaven received
Into the bosom of the steady lake.

The first task of the poet – if I may proceed with my allegorization of this memorable passage – is to learn how to entwine his or her hands so that the whistle comes out right. This may seem a minimal achievement, yet those of you who have a memory of attempting to get it right will also remember the satisfaction and justification implicit in that primary sounding forth of one's presence. People who learned to whistle on their thumbs, to trumpet and tu-whit, tu-whoo in the back seats of classrooms and the back seats of buses, would then be happy to perform this feat for its own sake, repetitively, self-forgetfully and tirelessly. It was an original act of making, the equivalent in the oral/aural sphere of mud-pies in the tactile/plastic sphere and, as has been well observed, one of the chief pleasures of life is when I show you the mud-pies I have made and you show me the mud-pies you have made. In this trope, the little magazine can be understood as an echo of owl whistles or a gallery of mud-pie life, and many a poetic career begins and ends with poems which do no more than cry out in innocent primary glee, 'Listen, I can do it! Look how well it turned out! And I can do it again! See?'

Sylvia Plath's first book contains several poems of this kind, beautifully tuned, half-rhymed and assonantal. In them, her craft-conscious fingers are twined and lifted at a careful angle, and her poetic breath is evenly, deliberately exhaled. Of course, it is not the only kind of work in *The Colossus* but it is what is most immediately in evidence; on every page, a poet is serving notice that she has earned her credentials and knows her trade. Relish it along with me, she insinuates; isn't this well done? And it is indeed a pleasure to savour the dull, sea-clap music of a poem like 'Mussel Hunter at Rock Harbour':

I came before the water –
Colourists came to get the
Good of the Cape light that scours
Sand grit to sided crystal
And buffs and sleeks the blunt hulls
Of the three fishing smacks beached
On the bank of the river's

Backtracking tail. I'd come for
Free fish-bait: the blue mussels
Clumped like bulbs at the grass-root
Margin of the tidal pools.
Dawn tide stood dead low. I smelt
Mud stench, shell guts, gull's leavings;
Heard a queer crusty scrabble

Cease, and I neared the silenced
Edge of a cratered pool-bed.
The mussels hung dull blue and
Conspicuous, yet it seemed
A sly world's hinges had swung
Shut against me. All held still.
Though I counted scant seconds,

Enough ages lapsed to win
Confidence of safe-conduct
In the wary otherworld
Eyeing me. Grass put forth claws;
Small mud knobs, nudged from under,
Displaced their domes as tiny
Knights might doff their casques. The crabs

Inched from their pygmy burrows
And from the trench-dug mud, all
Camouflaged in mottled mail
Of browns and greens. Each wore one
Claw swollen to a shield large
As itself – no fiddler's arm
Grown Gargantuan by trade,

But grown grimly, and grimly
Borne, for a use beyond my
Guessing of it. Sibilant
Mass-motived hordes, they sidled
Out in a converging stream
Toward the pool-mouth . . .

This is a poem in syllabics, seven syllables to the line, seven lines to the stanza; it inches itself forward as the crabs do, as Ted Hughes said her poems did in the beginning, felicity by felicity. The movement is steady, onward, purposeful, yet we are also being encouraged to hesitate in this 'wavy otherworld' and to appreciate the slubbed texture of lines like 'the mussels hung dull blue and/ Conspicuous, yet it seemed/ A sly world's hinges had swung/ Shut against me.' We are invited to indulge the poet ever so slightly, to allow her to raise her eye a fraction from the level of crabs to the level of casques. Casque, a word chivalric, plump and metallic, takes our eye off the object for a millimoment. We are, of course, happy to be so richly distracted, and the poem is not so fanatically engaged with its own purposes that it has not the leisure to take us by the elbow and point us towards the riches of its own linguistic estate. Indeed, the reader's pleasure comes from just this sense of being on a linguistic tour where the point of the outing is as much to relish the guide's vocabulary as to see what is being talked about.

So the poem goes about its business which, like the crab's business, isn't 'fiddling'; but neither is it absolutely engaged until its final two stanzas. The second half of it goes on:

Stood shut out, for once, for all,
Puzzling the passage of their
Absolutely alien
Order as I might puzzle
At the clear tail of Halley's

Comet coolly giving my
Orbit the go-by, made known
By a family name it
Knew nothing of. So the crabs
Went about their business, which

[156]

Wasn't fiddling, and I filled
A big handkerchief with blue

Mussels. From what the crabs saw,
If they could see, I was one
Two-legged mussel-picker.
High on the airy thatching
Of the dense grasses I found
The husk of a fiddler-crab,
Intact, strangely strayed above

His world of mud – green colour
And innards bleached and blown off
Somewhere by much sun and wind;
There was no telling if he'd
Died recluse or suicide
Or headstrong Columbus crab.
The crab-face, etched and set there,

Grimaced as skulls grimace: it
Had an Oriental look,
A samurai death mask done
On a tiger tooth, less for
Art's sake than God's. Far from sea –
Where red-freckled crab-backs, claws
And whole crabs, dead, their soggy

Bellies pallid and upturned,
Perform their shambling waltzes
On the waves' dissolving turn
And return, losing themselves
Bit by bit to their friendly
Element – this relic saved
Face, to face the bald-faced sun.

Something really comes to life when we get to the husk of that
voyager beyond the herd's track, the 'headstrong Columbus
crab'. A change occurs in the poem's dominant undersong,
which until then has been a wind-strummed, wave-thumped
background throb. We move from pulse-beat to mind-flight,
the hardness of the shell being matched by a hardening and

brightening of the poem's weather. Concentration soars from the crustacean to the cerulean, the action quickens, the lines which until now had been absorbed in the propriety of their effects are suddenly athletically on the move: 'it/ Had an Oriental look,/ A samurai death mask done/ On a tiger tooth, less for/ Art's sake than God's.' This is more like speech and has an excited air, as if the poem has stopped trailing and come upon its find. In terms of the musical curve of the whole thing, it permits a resolution: the cadences can settle after this long awaited flare-up, short and odd though it may have been. In terms of the sensuous instincts, the poem's somnolent involvement with viscous, muddy, sluggish matters is released by the attainment of a hard-held shape, a rigid cast which saves 'Face, to face the bald-faced sun'. Psychologically, too, balance has been attained. Without reading the poem biographically, it is still possible to recognize that the otherworld of the shore – with all the 'mass-motivated horde' life of the crab-procession – constitutes a kind of limbo for the speaker, leaving her excluded, unattached and yet all the while expectant; so that when she discovers the shell and makes a connection with it as the emblem of a recluse or a suicide or an explorer, it represents a certain founding of identity and security. Naturally, however, this is a complex kind of security:

> The crab-face, etched and set there,
>
> Grimaced as skulls grimace: it
> Had an Oriental look,
> A samurai death mask done
> On a tiger tooth, less for
> Art's sake than God's. Far from sea –
> Where red-freckled crab-backs, claws
> And whole crabs, dead, their soggy
>
> Bellies pallid and upturned,
> Perform their shambling waltzes
> On the waves' dissolving turn
> And return, losing themselves
> Bit by bit to their friendly

Element – this relic saved
Face, to face the bald-faced sun.

The skull image, the death mask, are here strangely vital.
What is truly malignant is that sea full of 'claws/ And whole
crabs, dead, their soggy/ Bellies pallid and upturned', performing 'their shambling waltzes'. It is not necessary to know about
Sylvia Plath's 1953 suicide attempt and her intent enterprise of
self-renewal to discover in the conclusion of this poem a drama
of survival, the attainment of a dry, hard-won ledge beyond the
welter and slippage of Lethean temptations. And the convincing thing, poetically, is that all this is guaranteed by an energy
beyond that mustered by the individual will. It seems managed
'less for/ Art's sake than God's'. It is as if in obeying the dictates
of her imagination and fastening upon the dead crab, Plath is
orienting herself towards the dry hard pitch she will attain in
the end, in poems like 'Words'. The crab husk is an art shape
and a talisman, something we accept at a level deeper than the
beautifully presented 'mussels/ Clumped like bulbs'. These
latter were literary owl-calls made through the careful fingers,
but the crab husk awakens the owl-life in *us*, calls up answering
calls in the twilight of our psyche and brings the poem over into
the second level of poetic attainment which is implicit in
Wordsworth's narrative.

When the vale fills with the actual cries of owls responding to
the boy's art, we have an image of the classically empowered
poet, the one who has got beyond scale-practising, the one
who, as Wordsworth says in his Preface, rejoices in the spirit of
life that is in him and is delighted to contemplate similar
volitions and passions as manifested in the goings-on of the
universe. This represents the poetry of relation, of ripple-and-
wave effect upon audience; at this point, the poet's art has
found ways by which distinctively personal subjects and
emotional necessities can be made a common possession of the
reader's. This, at its most prim, is a matter of the old 'what oft
was thought but ne'er so well expressed' kind of thing. At its
most enriching, it operates by virtue of skeins of language
coming together as a dream-web which nets psyche to psyche
in order to effect what Frost called 'a clarification', 'a momen-

tary stay against confusion' – precisely the kind of moment which occurs at the end of 'Mussel Hunter at Rock Harbour'.

Ted Hughes has written about Sylvia Plath's breakthrough into her deeper self and her poetic fate: he locates the critical moment in her writing at the composition of the poem called 'Stones'. This is the latest of the poems (4 November 1959) printed in *The Colossus*, and the one which we can with hindsight recognize as promising those epoch-making *Ariel* poems that began to arrive in October 1962. Between these two moments, the gravid yield of poems subsequently collected in *Crossing the Water* was written; and also the following, collected in *Ariel* but composed before the big spasm of poems in October 1962: 'Elm', 'The Moon and the Yew Tree', 'Tulips', and 'Morning Song'. These, together with 'The Bee Meeting' and 'The Arrival of the Bee Box', and poems from *Crossing the Water* like 'Parliament Hill Fields', 'In Plaster', 'Wuthering Heights', 'Blackberrying', 'Finisterre', 'Last Words', 'Mirror', 'Crossing the Water', 'Among the Narcissi', and 'Pheasant', belong to a phase of Sylvia Plath's art which holds in happy equilibrium the recognized procedures of what Eliot called 'the mythic method', and the terrible stresses of her own psychological and domestic reality. In this middle stretch of her journey, she practises the kind of poem adumbrated by Pound – in Canto I, for example – in which a first voice amplifies the scope of its utterance by invoking classical or legendary parallels. These poems are serenely of their age, in that the conventions of modernism and the insights of psychology are relayed in an idiom intensely personal, yet completely available. When we read, for example, the opening lines of 'Elm', the owls in our own dream branches begin to halloo in recognition:

I know the bottom, she says. I know it with my great tap root:
It is what you fear.
I do not fear it: I have been there.

In his edition of the *Collected Poems*, Ted Hughes provides a note to 'Elm', and an earlier draft from which this deeply swayed final version emerged. There are still twenty-one work-sheets to go, so the following represents only what Hughes calls 'a premature crystallization'. (The wych-elm which occasioned

the poems grows on the shoulder of a moated prehistoric
mound outside the house where Plath and Hughes lived.)

> She is not easy, she is not peaceful;
> She pulses like a heart on my hill.
> The moon snags in her intricate nervous system.
> I am excited seeing it there
> It is like something she has caught for me.
>
> The night is a blue pool; she is very still.
> At the centre she is still, very still with wisdom.
> The moon is let go, like a dead thing.
> Now she herself is darkening
> Into a dark world I cannot see at all.

The contrast between this unkindled, external voice and the
final voice of 'I know the bottom, she says' is astonishing. The
draft is analytical and unaroused, a case of ego glancing around
on the surface of language. In fact, what Plath is doing here is
packaging insights she had arrived at in another definitive tree
poem called 'The Moon and the Yew Tree', a subject set by Ted
Hughes, who writes in his 'Notes on the Chronological Order
of Sylvia Plath's Poems':

> Early one morning, in the dark, I saw the full moon setting
> on to a large yew that grows in the churchyard, and I
> suggested she make a poem of it. By midday, she had
> written it. It depressed me greatly. It's my suspicion that
> no poem can be a poem that is not a statement from the
> powers in control of our life, the ultimate suffering and
> decision in us.

'Elm' clearly comes from a similar place, from the ultimate
suffering and decision in Sylvia Plath, but access to that place
could not occur until the right rhythm began to turn under her
tongue and the sentence-sounds started to roll like fly-wheels
of the poetic voice. The ineffectual wingbeats of 'The night is a
blue pool; she is very still./ At the centre she is still, very still
with wisdom', are like the bird of poetry at the glass pane of
intelligence, seeing where it needs to go but unable to gain
entry. But the window glass is miraculously withdrawn and

deep free swoops into the blue pool and into the centre are effected with effortless penetration once the new lines begin to run:

> Is it the sea you hear in me,
> Its dissatisfactions?
> Or the voice of nothing, that was your madness?
>
> Love is a shadow.
> How you lie and cry after it.
> Listen: these are its hooves: it has gone off, like a horse.

Here too is dramatic evidence of another mark of high achievement, the interweaving of imaginative constants from different parts of the *œuvre*. These hooves are related to the hooves of the runaway Ariel, just as they are also pre-echoes of the phantom hoof-taps of 'Words'.

The elm utters an elmy consciousness, it communicates in tree-speak: 'This is the rain now, this big hush'. But the elm speaks poet-consciousness also. What is exciting to observe in this poem is the mutation of voice; from being a relatively cool literary performance, aware of its behaviour as a stand-in for a tree, it gradually turns inward and intensifies. Somewhere in the middle, between a stanza like:

> I have suffered the atrocity of sunsets.
> Scorched to the root
> My red filaments burn and stand, a hand of wires

– between this immensely pleasurable mimesis and the far more disturbing expressionism of

> I am terrified by this dark thing
> That sleeps in me;
> All day I feel its soft, feathery turnings, its malignity

– between these two stanzas the poem has carried itself – and the poet, and the reader – from the realm of tactful, estimable writing to the headier, less prescribed realm of the inestimable. It is therefore no surprise to read in Ted Hughes's notes of 1970 that he perceives 'Elm' as the poem which initiates the final phase, that phase whose poems I attempted to characterize earlier as seeming to have sprung into being at the behest of some unforeseen but completely irresistible command.

I wish now to reapproach those last poems in terms of Wordsworth's passage. The third kind of poetry I find suggested there is that in which the poem's absolute business is an unconceding pursuit of poetic insight and poetic knowledge. We have passed the first stage where poetic making was itself an end and an anxiety; and we have come through the second stage of social relation and emotional persuasion, where the owl-cry of the poems stimulates the answering owl-dream in the audience and 'strikes . . . as a remembrance'. In terms of the Wordsworth story, we have arrived at the point where the boy cannot make any noise with his hands:

> . . . And, when there came a pause
> Of silence such as baffled his best skill:
> Then, sometimes, in that silence, while he hung
> Listening, a gentle shock of mild surprise
> Has carried far into his heart the voice
> Of mountain-torrents; or the visible scene
> Would enter unawares into his mind
> With all its solemn imagery, its rocks,
> Its woods, and that uncertain heaven received
> Into the bosom of the steady lake.

Here the boy – call him the poet – has his skill mocked; skill is no use any more; but in the baulked silence there occurs something more wonderful than owl-calls. As he stands open like an eye or an ear, he becomes imprinted with all the melodies and hieroglyphs of the world; the workings of the active universe, to use another phrase from *The Prelude*, are echoed far inside him. This part of the story, then, suggests that degree of imaginative access where we feel the poem as a gift arising or descending beyond the poet's control, where direct contact is established with the image-cellar, the dream-bank, the word-hoard, the truth-cave – whatever place a poem like Yeats's 'Long-Legged Fly' emerges from. What Sylvia Plath wrote in those days of somnambulist poetic certitude belong with that *kind* of poetry. There is an absoluteness about the tone, and a sudden in-placeness about the words and all that they stand for, as in the poem 'Edge'. This is perhaps the last she wrote, perhaps the second last, one of two completed on 5 February 1963, six days before her suicide:

> The woman is perfected.
> Her dead
>
> Body wears the smile of accomplishment,
> The illusion of a Greek necessity
>
> Flows in the scrolls of her toga,
> Her bare
>
> Feet seem to be saying:
> We have come so far, it is over.
>
> Each dead child coiled, a white serpent,
> One at each little
>
> Pitcher of milk, now empty.
> She has folded
>
> Them back into her body as petals
> Of a rose close when the garden
>
> Stiffens and odours bleed
> From the sweet, deep throats of the night flower.
>
> The moon has nothing to be sad about,
> Staring from her hood of bone.
>
> She is used to this sort of thing.
> Her blacks crackle and drag.

Here is an objectivity, a perfected economy of line, a swift surehanded marking of the time and space which had been in waiting for this poem. 'Boldness in face of the blank sheet', which Pasternak declared one of the attributes of talent, was never more in evidence. The firmed-up music of the writing, its implacably indicative mood, mimes the finality of the woman's death. Even though consoling images of grave goods and children enfolded as petals are given due admittance, the overall temperature is that of a morgue. The bone-hooded moon and the bare feet share a chilly sort of dead-weight factuality. Never were the demands of Archibald MacLeish's 'Ars Poetica' so thoroughly fulfilled:

> A poem should be palpable and mute
> As a globed fruit,
>
> Dumb
> As old medallions to the thumb . . .
>
> A poem should be equal to:
> Not true . . .
>
> A poem should not mean
> But be.

There is a mute, palpable, equal-to 'being' about 'Edge' which insists that we read it as a thing sufficient within itself, which it certainly is. But it is also problematically something else. A suicide note, to put it extremely. An act of catharsis and defence, maybe, or maybe an act of preparation. The 'being' of this poetry, in other words, is constantly being pressed with meanings that sprang upon it the moment Sylvia Plath died by her own hand. Even an image like the dead crab, strayed headstrongly beyond his fellows, is retrospectively canvassed to serve the plot of suicide's progress. I would prefer to read the crab image as I believe the poem wants us to read it: as a relic that saved face, a talisman which helped the protagonist to face the bald-faced sun, an earnest of art's positively salubrious resistance to the shambling pull of the death wish. I would also wish to contend that the most valuable part of the late Plath *œuvre* is that in which bitterness and the embrace of oblivion have been wrestled into some kind of submission or have been held at least in momentary equilibrium by the essentially gratifying force of the lyric impulse itself. A poem like 'Daddy', however brilliant a *tour de force* it can be acknowledged to be, and however its violence and vindictiveness can be understood or excused in light of the poet's parental and marital relations, remains, nevertheless, so entangled in biographical circumstances and rampages so permissively in the history of other people's sorrows that it simply overdraws its rights to our sympathy.

Considerations of this sort bring to mind an 'Ars Poetica' very different from MacLeish's, one which is pertinent not only to the consideration of Sylvia Plath's poetry but to the general theme of these lectures, submerged as the theme may have been for much of the time. To what extent should the tongue be in the control of the noble rider of socially responsible intellect, ethics or morals? I have, on the whole, inclined to give the tongue its freedom, saying of the Elizabeth Bishop poem that it most excelled when it exceeded its modesty and obedience, when it went over the top by going under the surface; commending Mandelstam for finding in Dante an example of unconstrained liberation; discovering in early Auden a phonetic otherness which established that earliest poetry as a standard against which his later work, however beautiful and humane, appeared more conventional and less compelled. In Lowell's case, I tried to argue that he appeased his moral being with acts of political protest, earning his poetic rights by service in the unpoetic world of jail; and I went on to say that the poems where his 'plotting' interferes least with the process are finally the most impressive.

I do not in fact see how poetry can survive as a category of human consciousness if it does not put poetic considerations first – expressive considerations, that is, based upon its own genetic laws which spring into operation at the moment of lyric conception. Yet it is possible to feel all this and still concede the justice of Czeslaw Milosz's rebuke to the autocracy of such romantic presumption. He has most recently outlined his objections in his book *The Estate of Poetry*, but 'Ars Poetica?' concentrates the case in a single poem:

I have always aspired to a more spacious form
that would be free from the claims of poetry or prose
and would let us understand each other without exposing
the author or reader to sublime agonies.

In the very essence of poetry there is something indecent:
a thing is brought forth which we didn't know we had in us,
so we blink our eyes, as if a tiger had sprung out
and stood in the light, lashing his tail.

That's why poetry is rightly said to be dictated by a daimonion,
though it's an exaggeration to maintain that he must be an
angel.
It's hard to guess where that pride of poets comes from,
when so often they're put to shame by the disclosure of their
frailty.

What reasonable man would like to be a city of demons,
who behave as if they were at home, speak in many tongues,
and who, not satisfied with stealing his lips or hand,
work at changing his destiny for their convenience?

It's true that what is morbid is highly valued today,
and so you may think that I am only joking
or that I've devised just one more means
of praising Art with the help of irony.

There was a time when only wise books were read
helping us to bear our pain and misery.
This, after all, is not quite the same
as leafing through a thousand works fresh from psychiatric
clinics.

And yet the world is different from what it seems to be
and we are other than how we see ourselves in our ravings.
People therefore preserve silent integrity
thus earning the respect of their relatives and neighbors.

The purpose of poetry is to remind us
how difficult it is to remain just one person,
for our house is open, there are no keys in the doors,
and invisible guests come in and out at will.

What I'm saying here is not, I agree, poetry,
as poems should be written rarely and reluctantly,
under unbearable duress and only with the hope
that good spirits, not evil ones, choose us for their instrument.

There is much here that fits the extreme case of Sylvia Plath.
Her last poems do present themselves with all the pounce and
irrefutability of a tiger lashing its tail. They are written under
unbearable duress and they do hope to be the instrument of

[*167*]

good spirits. They certainly register the difficulty she found in remaining one person, and a poem like 'Lady Lazarus' ultimately concentrates an identity in a heave of renewal, whereas 'Daddy' disperses it in a blast of evacuation. And there are other poems besides 'Daddy' which are morbid. Yet when we read late lyrics like 'Balloons', 'Kindness', 'Child', 'Sheep in Fog', 'The Night Dances', 'Nick and the Candlestick', and even one as empty of human consolation as 'Lyonesse', we are surely reading work by somebody who wrote with the hope that good spirits were choosing her for their instrument.

There is nothing *poetically* flawed about Plath's work. What may finally limit it is its dominant theme of self-discovery and self-definition, even though this concern must be understood as a valiantly unremitting campaign against the black hole of depression and suicide. I do not suggest that the self is not the proper arena of poetry. But I believe that the greatest work occurs when a certain self-forgetfulness is attained, or at least a fullness of self-possession denied to Sylvia Plath. Her use of myth, for example, tends to confine the widest suggestions of the original to particular applications within her own life. This is obviously truer at the beginning of her career, and does not apply to such first-hand 'mythic' occasions as 'Elm'. Nevertheless her clued-in literary intelligence never quite ceased to inspect the given emotional and biographical matter for its translatability into parallel terms of literature or legend. In a poem like 'Ariel', the rewards are patent: the original allusion both swallows and is swallowed by the autobiographical occasion, and there is no sense of one element commandeering the other. In 'Lady Lazarus', however, the cultural resonance of the original story is harnessed to a vehemently self-justifying purpose, so that the supra-personal dimensions of knowledge – to which myth typically gives access – are slighted in favour of the intense personal need of the poet.

But even as one searches for a way to express what one senses as a limitation, one remembers this poet's youth and remembers also that it was precisely those 'intense personal needs' which gave her work its unprecedented pitch and scald. Her poems already belong to the tradition not just because they fulfil the poetic needs I outlined at the beginning – those considerations of tone, speech and dramatic enactment – but because they are also clearly acts of her being, words from which, in Buber's terms, effective power streams. They demon- ✓ strate the truth of Wordsworth's wonderful formulation, in his 1802 Preface to *Lyrical Ballads*, of the way poetic knowledge gets ✓ expressed. Wordsworth's account is the finest I know of the problematic relation between artistic excellence and truth, between Ariel and Prospero, between poetry as impulse and poetry as criticism of life. The following quotation includes a perhaps over-familiar sentence, and may show some syntactical strain, but it covers a lot of the essential ground:

> Not that I mean to say, that I always began to write with a distinct purpose formally conceived; but I believe that my habits of meditation have so formed my feelings, as that my description of such objects excite those feelings, will be found to carry along with them a *purpose*. If in this opinion I am mistaken, I can have little right to the name of a poet. For all good poetry is the spontaneous overflow of powerful feelings: but though this is true, poems to which any value can be attached, were never produced on any variety of subjects but by a man, who being possessed of more than usual organic sensibility, had also thought long and deeply. For our continued influxes of feeling are modified and directed by our thoughts, which are indeed the representatives of all our past feelings; and, as by contemplating the relation of these general representatives to each other we discover what is really important to men, so by the repetition and continuance of this act, our feelings will be connected with important subjects, till at length, if we be originally possessed of much sensibility, such habits of mind will be produced, that, by obeying blindly and mechanically the impulses of those habits, we shall describe objects, and utter sentiments, of such a nature and in such connection with each other, that the understanding of the being to whom we address our- selves, if he be in a healthful state of association, must necessarily be in some degree enlightened, and his affec- tions ameliorated.

Essentially, Wordsworth declares that what counts is the quality, intensity and breadth of the poet's concerns between the moments of writing, the gravity and purity of the mind's appetites and applications between moments of inspiration. This is what determines the ultimate human value of the act of poetry. That act remains free, self-governing, self-seeking, but the worth of the booty it brings back from its raid upon the inarticulate will depend upon the emotional capacity, intellectual resource and general civilization which the articulate poet maintains between the raids.

For permission to reproduce from the following copyrighted material the
publisher gratefully acknowledges:

Random House, Inc., for "The Shield of Achilles," "Venus Will Now
Say a Few Words," "The Watershed," "Taller To-day," "A Summer
Night," "Thank You, Fog," "Autumn Song," and "The Fall of Rome"
from Collected Poems by W. H. Auden, edited by Edward Mendel-
son, copyright © 1976 by Edward Mendelson, William Meredith, and
Monroe K. Spears, Executors of the Estate of W. H. Auden; Harcourt
Brace Jovanovich, Inc., for "The Love Song of J. Alfred Prufrock,"
"The Waste Land," and "Gerontion" from Collected Poems 1909–
1962 by T. S. Eliot, copyright 1936 by Harcourt Brace Jovanovich,
Inc., copyright © 1963, 1964 by T. S. Eliot; The Ecco Press for "Eschatological Forebodings of Mr. Cogito," "Damastes (Also Known As
Procrustes) Speaks," "The Divine Claudius," "Mr. Cogito—Notes
from the House of the Dead," and "Report from the Besieged City"
from Report from the Besieged City and Other Poems by Zbigniew Herbert, translated by John and Bogdana Carpenter, copyright ©
1985 by Zbigniew Herbert; The Ecco Press for "Apollo and Marsyas,"
"Pebble," and "A Knocker" from Selected Poems by Zbigniew Her-
bert, translated by Czeslaw Milosz and Peter Dale Scott, copyright ©
1968 by Zbigniew Herbert, translation copyright © 1968 by Czeslaw
Milosz and Peter Dale Scott; Oberlin College Press for "Teacher," "The
Corporal Who Killed Archimedes," "Man Cursing the Sea," and "The
Fly" from Sagittal Section: Selected and New Poems by Miroslav
Holub (FIELD Translation Series), translated by Stuart Friebert and
Dana Habova, copyright © 1980 by Oberlin College; Penguin Books
Ltd. for "Zito the Magician" from Selected Poems by Miroslav
Holub, translated by Ian Milner and George Theiner, copyright © 1967
by Miroslav Holub, translation copyright © 1967 by Penguin Books
Ltd.; Mrs. Katherine B. Kavanagh (c/o Peter Fallon, Loughcrew, Old-
castle, Co. Meath, Ireland) for "Innocence," "Canal Bank Walk,"
"Spraying the Potatoes," "In Memory of My Mother," "Auditors In,"
The Great Hunger, and "Prelude" from Collected Poems by Patrick
Kavanagh, copyright © 1964 by Patrick Kavanagh; Harcourt Brace Jo-
vanovich, Inc., for "The Quaker Graveyard in Nantucket" from Lord
Weary's Castle by Robert Lowell, copyright 1946 and renewed 1974
by Robert Lowell; Princeton University Press for "Poem 78," "Poem
53," and "Poem 62" from Stone by Osip Mandelstam, translated by
Robert Tracy, copyright © 1981 by Princeton University Press; The
Ecco Press for "Incantation," "Child of Europe," and "Ars Poetica?"
from Collected Poems 1931–1987 by Czeslaw Milosz, copyright ©
1988 by Czeslaw Milosz Royalties, Inc.; Oxford University Press, New
York, for "The Interrogation" from Collected Poems by Edwin Muir,
copyright © 1960 by Willa Muir; Harper and Row, Inc., for "Words,"
"Elm," and "Edge" from Collected Poems by Sylvia Plath, edited by Ted
Hughes, copyright © 1960, 1965, 1971, and 1981 by the Estate of Sylvia
Plath; Alfred A. Knopf, Inc., for "Mussel Hunter at Rock Harbor" from
The Colossus by Sylvia Plath, copyright © 1958 by Sylvia Plath.